Santa and the Business of Being Santa
"Santa and the Performing Santa"

An Introduction to Story Telling,
Magic, Stage Presence,
Improvisation, Song. and
Character Development and Role Portrayal
Through the Exploration into the History of the
Christmas Traditions,
and the Formative Influences
Of the Santa Character

Workbook Vol. 3

By

Santa Bertram "Gordon" Bailey

"If you can't dazzle them with your brilliance

Or bury them under your command of the subject,

Blind them with Bovine Excrement."

ISBN-13: 978-1547000234
ISBN-10: 1547000236

Published by **North Pole Publishing House**
in cooperation with

Fabled Santa – Santa Stephen Arnold
Fabled Santa Industries
1779 Kirby Pkwy #1-114
Memphis, TN 38138
SATBOBS@FabledSanta.com

North Pole

PUBLISHING HOUSE

4726 Stage Rd • Suite 101 • Memphis TN 38128
NORTHPOLEPUBLISHINGHOUSE.COM

About the Author

Santa Gordon Bailey, owner and head instructor for the Santa and the Business of being Santa School, has been a professional Santa Claus for over thirty-four years. Additionally, he is a trained Clown, experienced performing Magician and a talented balloon artist.

- Just some of his experiences include:
- Member of AORBS through 2008, FORBS through 2012,and IBRBS from 2012 to present
- Nationwide Santas Member # R1
- Lecturer for IUSC from the first class held at U.S.C.
- Double lecturer at Branson 2006
- Lecturer for FORBS reunion luncheons through 2012
- Lecturer for FORBS regional luncheon 2013
- Contributing author to the Magic Castle Library
- Lecture topics include Performance Parlor Magic, Close-up Magic, Walk around magic, Magic Performance, Animal Balloons, Face painting, Clowning, Impromptu and Improvisational perform-ance, Comedy, Make up application for Clowns, Trauma simulation make up, Life style differences between 15th century peasantry and 21rst century America. Multiple topics relating to performing as Santa.
- Performed as a Clown, Magician, Wizard, Pirate, Ogre, Face Painter, Balloon artist, Story Teller, and Santa since 1981.

Table of Contents

Foreword

This is the third textbook for the "Santa and the Business of being Santa" Santa school.

The focus of this volume is to help you learn about the art of performance working in intimate personal interaction with your audience. The subjects discussed will cover Performance Magic suitable in a Santa theme, Improvisation, Story Telling, Stage Presence, Song, Character and role development and how to bring these diverse subjects together into a comprehensive presentation of "Santa".

Volume one, "Santa and the Business of being Santa" deals with the business of being an Independent Contractor Entertainer.

Volume two, "Santa and the Nuts & Bolts of being Santa" deals with the connections you will need to the businesses and people that support and hire us to portray that role.

When combined, the three volumes make up the base of the traveling Santa School "Santa and the Business of being Santa" but these books are also "Stand Alone" texts that will help you even if you never set foot in any Santa class. I hope you enjoy and benefit from these writings in your pursuit of becoming a Professional Performer and Santa.

All three of these textbooks have gone through the process of updating the information and are now "Second Edition" with expanded material.

Dedication

This book is dedicated to all the performers I learned from along the path of my life. First of these would be some of the childhood television stars I later met and learned from in person. Bev Bergeron, Mark Wilson, Harry Blackstone Jr. gave many of us our first taste of Magic through the small screen.

Just as important were the "working" performers that did not appear on the small screen but were much more involved with the type of performance this book is about, that of fully interactive public performance. Some you may have heard of others, perhaps not but all shared their knowledge with me and before I pass this work on to you, I would have you remember their names. In no particular order: Karrell Fox, Dr. Bob Doggett, Marvin Roy, Claudia Munoz, Carmen Tellez, Rebecca Werner-Turner, Kitty Fisher, Gina Bacon, Carol Turner, Abb Dickson, Harlan Tarbell through his extensive writings, Jonathan Hillmer, Andy Roy, Steve Sutherland, Mick Foley, Sandee Gee, Cheri Serna, Suds Sudbreck, Tim Connaghan, Ian Loxton, Bob McMasters, Stephen Arnold, Tom Cortemeglia, Stephen Hollen, Blair Bell, Kristi Peters, Sam Sidoti, Robert Seutter, Charles Barnett, Ron Vedder, Judy Kidney and many more. This book stands upon the information shared by these wonderful performers and many more too numerous to mention but all have added to this presentation. I share my experience now with you before my memory dims.

Flowers for Algernon.

How to use this Book

You will be "roleplaying" the character of Santa Claus and so you will need some of this information to make your portrayal "Real" for the audience. Performing a character is much more than putting on a suit and boots. You must "put on" the character as well.

Imagine portraying President Lincoln without knowing the details of his life and deeds. At best you would be President Lincoln with Amnesia or extreme dementia.

Part of taking on a role is learning all there is to know about the history of the character and the times he or she lived in.

The more you know about the minutia, the personal habits, the company kept, the successes and the failures, all the Details and overall History of the character you are trying to portray, the more lifelike and "real" your character portrayal will be for your audience.

So having as much information as you can is a way to bring your portrayal to "life" in the eyes of your audience. This book will provide you with a basic background into the History of the Character called "Santa" and some of the Influences and Traditions that shaped the way he is presented today.

Take the details that suit you and your image of the Character and weave them into your own personal background story line for your presentation.

Start off with the facts and details you are comfortable with but the more you incorporate into that background, even if you never use it in a performance, the better your performance will become. Learn about the life and deeds of St. Nicholas as the character is based in part upon them. Learn about the "Other" Saint and all the other pre-Christian Gift Givers that were absorbed into our modern Christmas Celebration Traditions as well.

Knowing the History and timeline will keep it in the background of your mind as you are performing. Remember that a "Live Performance" does not always follow your Script and you need to be able to adapt to those questions and visitors that throw a monkey wrench into your well planned and carefully crafted presentation.

I have run across many of those "What the heck do I say now?" moments during my career as a Professional Santa and having those Histories and bullet point factoids have allowed me to regain control of the performance while remaining in Character.

When all else fails, stroke your mustache, look up for a moment, stroke your beard, look down for a moment and tug your beard. If that has not given you enough time to formulate an answer, fall back on "I will have to ask Mrs. Claus about that and get back to you." Then go back and do more research.

Building a Santa Visit Program
How a prepared program can make you more versatile performer.

One of the most valuable skills you can learn as a Santa is storytelling. Not only is it well received by your audience both children and adults alike, it also adds another dimension to the Santa character you are portraying. I say dimension because so many new Santas have very little depth to their portrayal.

As a new Santa, the more facets or dimensions you bring to your presentation, the greater the chance your audience will accept you as "Real" and the greater enjoyment they will derive from that performance. Look at it this way; a Magician strives to help you suspend your disbelief so you believe that magic is real. Otherwise he is just a guy doing tricks and nobody likes to be "tricked".

If your research is limited to the Rankin Bass stop action "Claymation" movies depicting Santa and life at the North Pole, then YOU will be a Claymation-stop action Santa. The more you dig into the character you are portraying the easier it is for your audience to suspend their disbelief and accept you as a "Real" Santa.

Just so, the more skills you add to your presentation, the deeper your knowledge of the character you are portraying with all the various traditions and histories associated with the formation of the "Santa Claus" character, the more "Real" your performance becomes. This book will both help you become a better Story Teller and help you develop your program offering. By having a pre-designed story telling program in place, you will be better able to deal with unforeseen scheduling and timing problems that may (and often do) occur during your Visit/performance.

The Story Telling chapter will have points on "Line of Sight" and "Eye Contact" with your audience. Talking in "First Person" while you are relating the stories that "Happened" to You as you portray the character rather than referring to yourself in "Third Person", Voice Projection, Breath Control, Cadence, Rhythm, Vocal Inflection, Pitch, as well as when to pause, insert a personal anecdote or observation, this is known as "bridging". All are going to be touched on in this section along with some Story Telling etiquette.

We will look at how Stories "fit" together bridging from one to the next. How you can segue from one story into a song and back into a story again. What is a "song" but a story set to music?

We will also be looking at Christmas songs as bases for stories to be told as well as use them in exercises later in this part of the book. Just look around you! Look at the various decorations and tools that we as Santa use in our presentation! Look at the Tree in the room with you. Look at your Suit and the various items you have added to it as part of your visual presentation.

Each and every one of them has a background story waiting to be told! The Red Suit, the Bag, the Boots, the Belt, the Gloves, the Hat, the Decoration on the Hat, the Small Bag hanging from the Belt or the Pouch on the Belt, the Bells you ring…All of these and anything else you might carry or wear while performing are stories waiting to be told. Truly the only limitation you have to your imagination is those you set upon yourself!

Performance as Santa

When you first decided to perform or "be" Santa your first thought was probably not to look in depth at all the methods and means of performing in front of a live audience. Most just put on the suit, stuff the bag and walk in the house. That first time.

Then you start to realize there is more to this than a Red Suit and a Jolly Ho Ho Ho! As I have stated many times, the best suit, shiniest boots, biggest beard, adding so many accessories that your knees buckle and a bag full of presents will only carry you through the first 5 minutes of a visit! After that, you have to have something more in the "bag of tricks" to pull out for the other 55.

So you will have to learn about "Stage Presence", Story Telling, Character Development and researching the character you are portraying in depth, possibly a little magic and do some study on the psychology of the visit. By the "psychology" of the visit I mean what the audience (children and adults) are going to react to in your presentation and how they will react when you perform can be predicted by studying Audience Psychology to give you an edge in the crafting of your presentation. You will be under a magnifying glass the entire time you are working and performing.

Your posture and how you sit, your manner of speaking and what you say as well as what you do not say, all of your gestures, both Large and Dramatic as well as facial and body language (micro-tells) will be under close scrutiny for your entire visit.

The more energy and personal effort you put into this effort before you even step through the door, the better and more believable your presentation will be. You will have to do a little study and research but as you learn your portrayal will improve and that leads to more and better events to book. I will start with some basic items and then we will get into more advanced concepts.

First thing you do is put on your suit and examine yourself in the mirror. What do you see? Is your hair neat and groomed? Beard too? How much hair is coming out of your ears and nose? Did you style your beard and mustache today? Are your boots polished? Is your suit clean? Gloves clean as well?

When you speak do you make gestures with your hands? How is your standing posture? Is your back straight and in line stacked with your pelvis and shoulders inline?

When you enter the room/home do you stride in like you are marching and in a hurry? Do you walk in casually but with awareness of those around you?

Is your head up and are you scanning the room making eye contact with the people in the room?

Do you acknowledge each of the people present with your gaze? Usually you are lead into the room from the front door by whoever opened the door.

Sometimes this is a child and sometimes it is an adult. Do you engage them in conversation loud enough for people to hear you? Do you project your voice and direct it at the various people you are visiting? Do you adjust your pace and gait to that of the child escorting you in?

Once you have found the "chair", how is your posture? Are you back in the chair or sitting forward? Again check your posture. Are your shoulders up and is your sitting posture forward? Is your body language and facial expression saying the same message? Both should be "open" and should say, "I am friendly and approachable!" Start out doing this well before season in front of a mirror so you can see what the audience sees. Make the changes needed and practice until it is second nature.

Make sure your smile reaches your eyes! Open your eyes wider than you would normally, especially when there is photography being done! It is natural to let your eyes be half closed but that does not look well in pictures. Eyes wide open gives a picture of you that is open and interested in what is going on around you.

Practice your smile in the mirror as well. Make your mouth curve upward and again, make sure that your eyes are part of that smile! Practice your thoughtful look as well.

Cultivate the habit of playing with your beard. Your beard is one of the defining characteristics of the character you are portraying! Draw attention to it! Smooth it and straighten it occasionally. Stroke it and play with it while you formulate answers to questions not on your "ready list". This gains you time to come up with a thoughtful answer. By spending time in this activity in front of a mirror you will define your "Santa" character and by adding this "menu" of facial expressions and gestures you become more into character. Always remember to be active and animated as you conduct your visit. This does not mean be hyper or constantly moving. Learn to modulate your voice and vocal expressions when talking in character. Unless "reading" a story and keeping to how it was written, keep all your personal references in the First person. Make sure your body language is open and friendly to all. In the following chapters, you will learn more about basic performance craft but it all starts with character development.

Constructing a Story Telling Program

Find a good starting point for your Story Telling segment. I use an original Story to do this called "My First Name" which is included in this book for your use.

When telling a story that is not your own creation, it is good Story Telling manners to credit the original author before reciting the work. Thus if you tell "The Night before Christmas" you should give credit to Clement C. Moore before going into the story. So if you decide to use any of the stories found here that originate from me, simply say this was written by Gordon Bailey thus giving me credit for my small contribution to the genre.

My program example starts with "My First Name" and that covers why I wear a suit without pockets (Traditional) and always carry a bag while tying into the ST. Nicholas Origin. I then go into some of the Old World "Traditions" that helped shape the modern day Santa image which leads into "The Night before Christmas".

After "The Night before Christmas" with the naming of the 8 reindeer, the children usually ask "What about Rudolf?" and after explaining that Rudolf came 110 years after the time of Mr. Moore, we sing "Rudolf the Red Nosed Reindeer". I always ask if the children know the name of the 10th reindeer. I point out it was in the song just sung. After some shouted answers, I tell them "Olive" as in "Olive, the other reindeer, used to laugh and call him names".

From this point we can move to one of several stories you can purchase from Amazon such as "The Longest Wish List" or "The Christmas Pumpkin" along with any of the stories you like from the actions accredited to St. Nicholas such as the one about the "Three Sisters" where St. Nicholas saved them from being sold into slavery by giving them a dowry.

I prefer to use my own stories simply because they have had so little exposure to the greater audience. One of my favorites is "The Elves, Mrs. Claus and Treats" which has a good lesson about eating your vegetables. I also like the short story I spun around "Mrs. Claus" and why next to her, you are light as a feather! That last developed mainly as an icebreaker to get grandmothers to sit on my knee for the picture. I found it worked all too well!

I like to finish with Robert Frost's poem "Stopping by the Woods on a Snowy Evening" as it makes a great closer!

"The woods are lovely, dark and deep

But I have promises to keep

And miles to go before I sleep

And miles to go before I sleep."

You should select your stories and put them together carefully. Try to keep each story down to less than 5 minutes each. All of the stories and songs I use are between 2 and 5 minutes in length.

The reason for this is to keep the program moving along and keep the attention of the younger children focused. For this reason I do not use the "Polar Express" even though it is a very fine story. When you begin building your program, time how long it takes you to tell each story. This allows you to keep track of time as you do the program since you know how long each story is and how many stories you tell will add up to the desired length of time. For instance:

"My First Name"   5 minutes

"Traditions"   3 minutes

 "The Night before Christmas"   4 minutes

"Rudolf the Red Nosed Reindeer" 3 minutes

"The Longest Wish List"   4 minutes

"The Elves, Mrs. Claus and Treats" 3 minutes

"Mrs. Claus"   2 minutes

"Stopping   by   the   Woods"   3   minutes

This program can run 30 minutes or even longer simply by plugging in more songs and stories or shortened to as little as 3 to 5 minutes depending upon the situation. Since it is modularized you can add to the program as needed or as circumstances apply.

Another reason for keeping the stories short is you can end the story telling segment at will without risk of not finishing the story in progress. For instance the family you had to stretch the program for arrived as you started the latest segment. That means you can now go on to the gift giving segment of the program without delay once you finish the story your telling and move on with the visit program.

Take the time to read and familiarize yourself with the stories you will be using before season starts. By doing this you shake out some of the rust accumulated since the end of last season. By your second or third performance you will be back in the groove with your story telling program.

Original Story offerings

My First Name

" What name or names do your know me by?" [The answers usually are] "Santa! Santa Claus! Kris Kringle! Old St Nick!" [The answers usually slow after this] "Oh I have many names! You probably know me best by "Santa" or Santa Claus" and some of you might know me as Kris Kringle derived from yet another German name "Kristkindl" which means "the Christ Child" and of course St. Nick" which comes from St. Nicholas."

"In other countries I have different names! In England I am known as 'Father Christmas'. In Germany I am known as 'Father Winter'. In Russia I am known as 'Father Frost'. In France I am called 'Pere Noel' and in Holland they call me 'SinterKlaas' and I have many more names around the world."

"But my first name was Nicholas. Now Nicholas was a real, living person who was born in 270 A.D. and passed away December 6th, 343. That was over 1670 years ago! Coincidentally, that is how old I am. We know of Nicholas because many of his deeds and works were documented and recorded back then."

"Nicholas was born to a couple late in their life. He was not expected but he was loved and cherished by his parents."

"His parents were merchants and in those times they had to travel to buy and sell their wares. One day on such a trip, they became ill and died, leaving Nicholas an orphan. So Nicholas was raised in an orphanage by monks. Nicholas was so impressed by how the monks treated the children under their care, he decided to become a monk himself and so became the youngest monk of his order." "As a monk, Nicholas lived and worked in a monastery that was in the land of Myra, which we now call Turkey today. Now a monastery is a large building with a sturdy wall that surrounds it on all 4 sides. The monks worked in the nearby town and surrounding farms and orchards."

(For those of you that don't know what a monk is, a monk is a religious person like a minister or a priest but instead of giving sermons in a church, monks worked side by side with the people of the lands and town they lived near. There are Monk bakers, and monk candle makers, and monk wine makers and monk farmers...) and as they worked they spread the word of God."

"The monastery was where you went to learn your letters and numbers. If you were injured or sick, you would go to the monastery to be made whole and well."

"Because of the large building and strong walls surrounding it, the monastery was a place of shelter and safe haven in times of strife."

"The Guild Masters and Town Leaders liked having all the benefits of the monastery nearby but they did not like their workers distracted by talk of religion. So they passed a law stating no one should speak of religious matters unless within the confines of 4 walls."

"Thinking that would keep the benefits of having the monastery nearby without any distractions from the monks.

Nicholas did not like this new law! He wanted to talk to anyone anytime about anything, much like any of you I suspect."

"So Nicholas spent an entire summer sewing up bags and into these bags he placed dried fruit, nuts, honeycomb, dried flowers and a few coins. Then at the winter solstice, Nicholas would knock on doors. To whoever answered the door, Nicholas would give the gift of a bag."

"In the middle of winter in that part of the world back then, food was very scarce so the dried fruit, nuts and honeycomb were greatly appreciated! The dried flowers remind them of the coming of spring and so gave a message of hope. Of course the coins were always appreciated! But it was the bag itself that was the most highly prized item!"

"Do you know why? Back then, pockets had not been invented yet! If you went to market to buy or sell something, you had to carry it in your hands, put it in your hat, or if you had a bag you could carry much more!"

"So overwhelmed by the gift of the bag, people would invite Nicholas inside and there within the confines of four walls, he could talk about anything he chose. Thus Nicholas spread the word of God. Now Nicholas lived a long life spanning 73 years with many accomplishments and adventures. He became the "Boy Bishop" and helped many people along the way of his life."

"When at last Nicholas passed away he was canonized. (Do you know what that means? They shot him out of a canon! ... NO! They made him a Saint!) And so Nicholas became St. Nicholas and that became my first name!"

"That is also why Santa has no pockets in his suit and why Santa always carries a bag."

The Elves, Mrs. Claus and Treats

"Before I tell you this story, there are 2 things you need to know. First, the youngest elf at the North Pole working in the Toy Shop is over 175 years old! Now that is very young for an Elf but very old for a human. Secondly, I don't know the rule in your home but at the North Pole, if you bite into a cookie ...You have to finish it! Not my rule, Mrs. Claus does not like having half eaten treats sitting around where I might gobble them up. She says it would spoil my appetite."

"Most likely you have not heard this story before because it only happened recently. We had a small problem at the North Pole. You see, the Elves stopped eating their vegetables! They only wanted to eat cookies and pies, Cakes and candy. The basic four food groups for Elves. While this did give the Elves a 'Sugar rush' and spiked production for a while, there were some draw backs to this behavior of the Elves. You see, when you're over 175 years old and you stop eating your vegetables, you get a little cranky. Not a good thing!"

"So Mrs. Claus and I put our heads together and tried to come up with a solution. And Mrs. Claus came up with the answer! She baked them into cookies!

Have you ever had a Peanut butter, Oatmeal, Chocolate chip, Lima Bean, Brussel Sprout cookie? Well they are kind of chewy! Eeeww? Have you ever tried one? No? Well you can't say 'Eeeww' then, can you?"

"Remember the rule? Bite into a cookie and you have to finish it? Well, Mrs. Claus put a BIG platter of those Peanut Butter, Oatmeal, Chocolate chip, Lima Bean, Brussel Sprout cookies out on that day and the Elves simply pounced on them! Almost at once, we had a lot of Elves going around with their cheeks puffed out like chipmunks and we went through a LOT of milk that day! "

"But then the Elves stopped eating the cookies so Mrs. Claus whipped up a delightful batch of double Chocolate fudge, Walnut, Asparagus brownies! After that, the Elves decided to start eating their vegetables so they could enjoy their treats the normal way. Without the vegetables. But I kind of got used to those Peanut butter, Oatmeal, Chocolate chip, Lima Bean, Brussel Sprout cookies so Mrs. Claus makes me a batch every now and then."

Mrs. Claus and why next to her, you're as light as a feather!

Once in a while, occasionally, ever so often, a lady will be shy about sitting on Santa's knee! Now no one should ever have reservations about this! After all! You only get the chance once a year!

They will say things like "I am too heavy!" or "I'll break your knee!" This story will give your adults a chuckle and ease them onto your knee for that picture.

"You're too HEAVY?!? Why next to Mrs. Claus you are light as a feather! Now when I first met Mrs. Claus, she was what you would call today a "Hottie" as she only weighed 115 pounds.

Now I have always appeared as what you see me today (waves hands about my person) but this young lady saw something in me that she wanted, and so she pursued my affections relentlessly until finally I gave in and consented to be married. Yup! My days a single Claus were at an end!

I must say that a strong and stable relationship is not based upon the physical appearance of the person one marries.

People change! I will admit I got the better end of the bargain as far as I could see though! Now I love Mrs. Claus dearly and we have had a very good and stable relationship throughout our time together but you see, Mrs. Claus turned out to be the BEST cookie maker EVER!

She spends all her days in the kitchen baking cookies! That is unless she isn't helping organizing the Elves or getting me ready for my ride around the world.

Oh! The varieties and flavors she makes are endless! However, Mrs. Claus is a "taster" in the kitchen and she has gained a little weight.

Now in her defense, Mrs. Claus only gained 1 pound a year and a stable and mutually respectable marriage partnership is not based on looks alone! God knows I love Mrs. Claus for who she is but the cookies are a nice bonus indeed!

Of course we have been married over 800 years now….So that is why I say "Next to Mrs. Claus you are light as a feather!" Ho Ho Ho!"

Story Telling Exercises

How having the opportunity to practice pays off in seasonal performance

When you first start to approach story telling as an activity to include in your presentation, start out at home with a voice recorder handy. Read your story while recording and then play it back to hear yourself.

Start out with a classic like "The Night before Christmas" and read it out loud. If you have not memorized the work before hand, chances are you will be surprised at how "flat" your voice will sound.

That is because you are concentrating on the written words rather on the story itself.

If you memorize the story before you attempt to "read" it, your performance will be much more lively and natural. Other ways to practice would be to volunteer to read to children at the public library or at a bookstore that offers such "readings" to the public.

For those of you lucky enough to have small children or grandchildren, you can have them sit for "story time" and get your practice in that way.

As you gain confidence and start to enjoy reciting your story, add new tales to your list of stories to tell. It is very important that you listen to your recorded voice to hear what you sound like regularly.

Learn to "Project" your voice by using your diaphragm and imagine your voice is coming from deeper in your throat down towards your chest. Learn to use your breath and control it when speaking to the public. Try opening your mouth a bit rounder and wider than you would normally. Play with your voice and exercise it just like any other tool or skill at your disposal.

Another exercise is to talk like you sing. Use your "Singing" voice to talk. It will take practice but these exercises will pay off when you perform!

When you sing, your voice will come from deeper in your throat while your normal speaking voice will seem to be coming from above your throat at the back of your mouth.

Normally your speaking voice will involve more of your nasal passages higher behind your nose while your singing voice will be far less nasal and far more rounded.

Always remember to use your diaphragm to force the air out and use your throat to focus and channel your voice. This is called "projection" and being able to project your voice will allow you to be heard without you raising your volume by shouting.

When you couple "Projecting" your voice with "Breath Control" you will notice a great improvement to your speaking voice and how people will react to you. If you sing you will notice that you speak normally in one octave and sing in a different octave(s). This is normal but when you learn to speak in your "Singing" voice you will then open up those different octaves to give you various "character" voices.

Lyrics for songs used as Stories

Dual usage storylines for reciting or singing

Just a little experiment that you might like to use in your program. Read them as straight stories, not as songs or poems and see how they might work in a story telling program. Look at other songs for similar use. You will find it a bit difficult to eliminate the Cadence and Rhythm of the "Song" as you "read" the story through. Once you can get past that, a whole new world opens up for you in storytelling.

Grandma Got Run Over By A Reindeer!

Grandma got run over by a reindeer walking home from our house Christmas Eve. You can say there's no such thing as Santa, but as for me and Grandpa, we believe!

She'd been drinking too much eggnog and we begged her not to go. But she forgot her medication so she staggered out the door and through the snow. When we found her Christmas morning at the scene of the attack, there were hoof-prints on her forehead and incriminating Claus marks on her back!

Now we're all so proud of Grandpa. He's been taking this so well. See him in there watching football? Drinking beer and playing cards with Cousin Mel. It's not Christmas without Grandma. All the family's dressed in black and we just can't help but wonder, should we open up her gifts or send them back?

Now the goose is on the table and the pudding made of fig. With the blue and silver candles that would just have matched the hair in Grandma's wig.

I warned all my friends and neighbors! Better watch out for yourselves! They should never give a license to a man who drives a sleigh and plays with elves!

Rudolf the Red Nosed Reindeer

You know Dasher and Dancer and Prancer and Vixen. Comet and Cupid and Donner and Blitzen. But do you recall, the most famous reindeer of all?

Rudolf the Red Nosed reindeer! He had a very shiny nose and if you ever saw it, you would even say it glows! All of the other reindeer used to laugh and call him names! They never let poor Rudolf join in any reindeer games.

Then one foggy Christmas Eve, Santa came to say "Rudolf with your nose so bright, won't you guide my sleigh tonight?"
Then all the reindeer loved him, as they shouted out with glee! Rudolf the Red Nosed reindeer! You'll go down in history!

God Rest Ye Merry Gentlemen

God rest ye merry gentlemen, let nothing you dismay! Remember, Christ our Savior was born on Christmas Day! To save us all from Satan's power when we were gone astray. O tidings of comfort and joy. Comfort and Joy! O tidings of comfort and joy.

In Bethlehem, in Israel, this blessed babe was born. And laid within a manger upon this blessed morn. The which his mother Mary did nothing take in scorn. O tidings of comfort and joy. Comfort and Joy! O tidings of comfort and joy.

From God our Heavenly Father a blessed angel came; and unto certain shepherds brought tidings of the same. How that in Bethlehem was born the Son of God by name! O tidings of comfort and joy. Comfort and Joy! O tidings of comfort and joy.

"Fear not then" said the Angel "Let nothing you affright, this day is born a Savior of a pure and Virgin bright! To free all those who trust in Him from Satan's power and might." O tidings of comfort and joy. Comfort and Joy! O tidings of comfort and joy.

The shepherds at those tidings rejoiced much in mind, and left their flocks a feeding in tempest, storm and wind: and went to Bethlehem straightway, The Son of God to find. O tidings of comfort and joy. Comfort and Joy! O tidings of comfort and joy.

And when they came to Bethlehem where our dear Savior lay. They found Him in a manger where oxen feed on hay. His mother Mary kneeling down unto the Lord did pray. O tidings of comfort and joy. Comfort and Joy! O tidings of comfort and joy.

Now to the Lord sing praises all you within this place. And with true love and brotherhood each other now embrace; this holy tide of Christmas all other doth deface. O tidings of comfort and joy. Comfort and Joy! O tidings of comfort and joy.

Using Props in Story Telling

Making use of visual properties to introduce and illustrate Story lines

Those of you that know me know that I am generally against the collection of the "latest bling" or adornment that hits the market but in certain cases, I will recommend including well thought out and well-crafted items such as this *Santa's Global Key*.

This particular prop is designed to engage the imagination of your visitors.

Starting from the "fob" end of the Key we have the decorative Celtic knots incorporated around the initials "SC". Four circles of Celtic knots representing the four seasons of the year with those initials in the center of the intersections of those circles. On the outside secondary points of the compass again where the circles intersect, are four nodal points.

All of which rests in turn upon a capital letter "W".

Below that there is the globe of the world where the "W" rests upon the representation of the North Pole. This Globe will remind you of the 60+ countries that have Christmas Traditions and Stories that are based on gift giving and St. Nicholas along with several other animals and creatures tied into the Christmas tradition as a whole.

The Globe in turn rests upon a fluted column that, at the opposite end of which are eight green gem stones that could represent the eight reindeer.

After this is on the barrel of the key are 3 large red stones that could represent the 3 wise men or the story of the three sisters St. Nicholas saved from slavery by providing a dowry so they could be married.

The "tooth" of the key features a cutout that could represent the Eastern Star that was followed by the 3 wise men or it could be the North Star or it could be a Compass Rose, all three of which were used in navigating.

The Compass Rose ties in with Sailors, Military and Pirates, all three of which St. Nicholas is the Patron Saint of.

Atop the end is a fine representation of Thor's Hammer. A symbol of the Winter Solstice / Christmas season for those of Norse decent.

Tying in with the "Odin" line of thought is the feature between the eight green stones and the three red stones. There is a "doughnut" with eight bumps on each side featured. That could tie into Odin's eight-legged horse named Sleipnir that he rode to bring gifts to the children.

Finally the barrel of the shaft represents the North Pole itself! Bringing us back to Santa's home!

So to recap the various story lines discovered in this one prop:

All of the rich story lines from the Celts and their history.

How Santa Claus covers the World.

The globe of the Earth and all the Cultural Stories from every country about Christmas.

The North Pole as shown by the Barrel of the key shaft, with all the stories that happen at Santa's home the rest of the year.

The Stories about the reindeer lead into by the eight green stones.

The three large red stones that tie into the Three Wise Men or The Three Sisters saved by St. Nicholas.

The "Star" in the tooth of the key that ties into the Eastern Star followed by the Three Wise Men, The North Star, and the Compass Rose used to navigate maps. The Compass Rose ties in with Sailors, Military men in uniform and Pirates. All three are under the patronage of St. Nicholas.

And finally, the tie in with the Norse Mythos of Odin as a gift bringer riding an eight-legged horse at the Winter Solstice.

At least 82 different story lines all in one small 6-inch gold plated Key. It is like having 82 different storybooks hanging off your belt waiting to be related to your audience at a moment's notice. With this device hanging from your belt, it is just one more decorative piece of your presentation but as we have seen, it is much more if you look at it with an eye toward storytelling.

Another example of "hidden" story suggestion lead offs is the "Miracle on 34th Street" styled *Reindeer buttons*. Each button has the name of two of the reindeer. They also have an image of a reindeer on each as well.

Since there are nine reindeer today, Rudolf is included but on that button with Rudolf's name is also "Santa". These buttons act the same way as in the Movie when interacting with the public. They generate open-ended questions that you can turn into a story telling opportunity and engage the children in flights of imagination! And, there is a sixth button that celebrates Mrs. Claus and Santa.

While I do not single out any one particular vendor, I do recommend you look for the highest quality manufacturing to add to your presentation whenever possible. Remember, this is a "long term" investment to your image presentation.

Sometimes the tradition is quite new and yet strikes a chord in the "Santa" story line/character background that it becomes a character support Prop that really has no story behind it beyond how it came to be. A Prop that fills a niche in the Santa presentation all year long that works as an "Ice Breaker" while supporting the idea that you are "Santa"!

I personally own one of the original *Bob King Badge and Wallet* and a Bob McMasters follow on Badge and Wallet. In the first year of ownership I have had nothing but smiles from everyone that has seen this tool. With the use of a "Santa license" in the window of the wallet this helps the

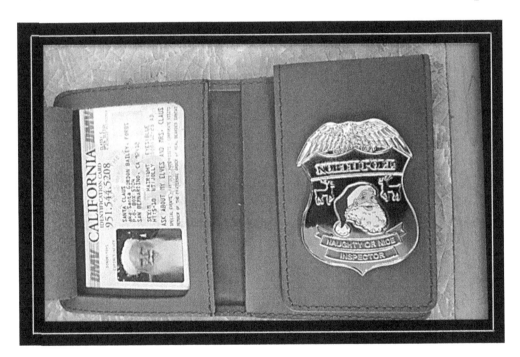

children decide it is proof that you are the "Official and Real Santa".

The following was written by Santa Bob McMasters (with some slight editing) about how this "Santa Badge and Wallet" came to be and where they can be found. It is generic in design and can be used by Santa, Mrs. Claus and Elves equally well.

This is a concerted effort to maintain some of the recent "TRADITIONS "we as Santa use. This is the Story and History behind Santa Bob King's Naughty or Nice Inspector Badge and Display Wallet. Written by Santa Bob McMasters on Wednesday, May 1, 2013.

Early in 2012, a Santa had an idea for a product that was very dear to his heart. He had researched and no one was offering his idea to the market. He further researched for a length of time and found a company that would take his idea and allow his design to be manufactured under his strict guidance as to the specifics of what he wanted at a fair price and meet his terms of quality.

This person, Santa Bob King, went forth with his idea for a Badge and Wallet to use in reinforcing his interaction with Children and Adults alike as Santa. What a great tool it turned out to be. So Santa Bob had the Badge and Wallet manufactured and brought to market in the summer of 2012.

After selling them for a very short time Santa Bob and his Wife Shirley took an Anniversary trip overseas and sadly enough He passed away while on their trip. Devastating those around him Family, Friends and the Santa Community alike.

This is where I come in for I was on Face Book and on a Santa Networking Page. There was Santa's asking about the Badge and Wallet.

I being friends with the Kings wrote Shirley with my condolences and asked her if she was going to continue to sell the Badge and Wallet and if it would be available for the 2012 Holiday Season.

She did not respond immediately but in January 2013 wrote me to say she was sorry for the delay in response and under the circumstances I fully understood for when I first wrote her she was still in grieving.

She explained she had a limited supply of the Badges and Wallets and now was ready to make them available again but only while supply lasted. And needless to say they were all depleted within a few days as the word of the quality of the pieces spread among the Santa Community.

I proposed to her at this time if she wasn't going to continue by reordering if I could take over the project and go a step further in honoring Santa Bob by naming them " The Santa Bob King's Naughty or Nice Inspectors Badge and Display Wallet ". She was very happy with this idea and in a public announcement turned the project over to me with her blessings and relayed the Company info over to me along with a list of those orders she could not fill. At that point the Badge and Wallet was priced and went into the manufacturing process. Everyone who received theirs from Mrs. King and from Me have spoken of the high quality of both pieces including myself and I am very proud of the product that one Santa was able to take from just an idea to a reality and I am Humbled and Honored to carry on Santa Bob King's vision of a tool for Santa's to use in everyday life to bridge the gap between Santa and those he touches in his travels and interactions each and every day.

It's is all about the Joy and Magic along with keeping the Spirit alive for Children and Adults alike!

Thank each and every one of those who already have or have placed orders for the one and only "Santa Bob King's Naughty or Nice Inspectors Badge and Display Wallet" ... SANTAcerely Bob McMasters .. Spreading Joy through Toys while keeping the Magic and Spirit and "Tradition "of CHRISTmas alive!

For anyone interested in owning their very own First of its kind and Original Naughty or Nice Badge and Wallet Honoring the late great Santa Robert D. " Bob " King the price is $38.00.

Side note, I personally have both versions of this Badge and Wallet. The Original Bob King in the black Wallet and the carried forward version manufactured by Bob McMasters in the red Wallet. Both are of equal high quality and have yet to have any other reaction but a smile from everyone I have shown it to from Children, Parents, Security metal detector check point Guards and even Texas State Troopers that pulled me over this last year. It has a pocket under the Badge that can hold your business cards and a clear window under a flap that can display your Santa License.

Combining a Visual Magic effect with Story Telling.
The Beginners Bible "Birth of Jesus" Story Cube

Pictured above is a "Story Cube" that tells a much abbreviated story of Mary and Joseph going to Bethlehem. It is 3 inches on a side and the fun thing about "reading" this cube is the way it opens and unfolds changing shape as it does only to return to a cube at the end ready to be "read" again. As "The Cube Unfolds… And So Does The Story!" It is a visual oddity and an entertaining difference from reading a book

The following section was written for me by Robert Seutter aka Santa True. Robert has been an experienced professional storyteller for over 27 years and he has graciously provided me with this level 400 treatise on performance and storytelling. Much of what he has to say is very important to beginning performers and I urge you to read it several times! It is reprinted here in the Performance book where it belongs.

The Performing Santa

"The highest compliment any Santa can get is when someone looks at you with wide eyes, no matter what age, and says, "Oh my God! You are the REAL Santa!"

— Santa True

When we decide to bring the iconic character of Santa to life, we are creating a character that has a great many expectations upon it. Everyone has their idea of what Santa is and is not, and how he should behave. Santa is larger than life, and by most expectations, should be excellent at everything he does. After all, he's a Saint, an Elf, possibly hundreds of years old, and magical to boot. He has almost unlimited wealth and a staff of thousands. He's magical, has the patience of a saint (original St. Nicholas not so much) and has a body of hundreds of songs, stories, books, and movies about him.

So when Santa is in front of the public or any audience, he has to both look good and sound good. For us mere mortals, bringing that character to life means bringing our A-game.

This is both a blessing and a curse. People want to believe in magic and the sense of wonder and play that Christmas and Santa bring. That's the blessing. The curse is that Santa is not allowed to have a bad day. Ever.

Today's Santa is often called on to be entertaining. This is especially true if you are a *Concierge Santa* (a termed coined by Storytelling Santa Stephen Hollen) or a *Performing Santa* —one who does home visits, corporate events, and parades to name a few. These scenarios often come with a different set of expectations than the typical "Photos with Santa" and the phrase, "What do you want for Christmas?"

As a performing Santa, you will need to have different skills and a variety of material to present. From the minute you make that entrance to the moment you leave, your job is to keep Santa magical and mythical, not to let Santa turn into an old guy with a beard sitting in a chair.

So let's look at some of the things we could be asked to do as performing Santas: Grand entrances, photo scenarios/posing, personal visits such as sitting on laps, asking and answering questions, recitations and readings, storytelling, singing and leading singing, magic, acting as an emcee, dancing, puppetry, playing musical instruments, show and tell, and question and answers. All of these have performance elements in common. Some elements rely on the one-on-one interaction, others play to a large audience, and some are geared toward to the intimacy of a camera.

Imagine if instead of delivering presents, Santa was a magical plumber. On December 24 as everyone went to sleep, he would fly to your house, jump out, fix all your leaky faucets, snake your drains, and install that new hot water heater you need so badly. Santa would need to have all the right tools. He would need some serious chops to deal with all the different plumbing scenarios. And he would certainly need to know about welding, copper pipes, and roto-rooters.

Now if I said to you; "Hi, we want you to be our plumbing Santa!" would you already have the skills to deal with those plumbing concerns? Some of us might say "Sure! I'm Morty the plumber in real life!" But most of us would say, "Sorry, that's why I hire a professional."

And just like this plumber example, some Santas are already professional performers. But most of us are not professional entertainers and have not come to the role of Santa through our entertaining background.

Certainly when we put on the Red Suit, as Santas we throw ourselves into the role. But this means that we might need some new skills in our toolkits. Just being a very good-looking Santa might not be enough.

In our example, Morty the plumber can usually train alongside another professional plumber for years. They can go to plumbing conventions, learn all the latest techniques, study for certifications, and even practice plumbing in their own shops and homes.

Unfortunately, having two Santas side-by-side is confusing and contrary to the current mythos of Santa. (Interesting side note: an early proto-Claus, the Belsnickels, often ran in packs) But in our role as Santa, we usually have to reinvent the wheel for ourselves, alone. We have very little peer feedback on the job, in the line of duty. And while there might be some excellent classes or workshops to attend at some Santa schools or reunions, there are almost no weekly Santa singing, storytelling, or public-speaking classes in our neighborhoods. And we rarely get a chance to practice being Santa in front of a live (but practice) audience. When we are

Santa with our clients, they expect us to be excellent because Santa is excellent. There are rarely any chances for a do-over.

Storytelling, Speaking, and Singing

Let's look at some of the foundational skills for storytelling, speaking, and singing. These are our building blocks for performing. For each of these, your voice is your primary tool. Second, your body and your physical skills come in to play. Part of being an excellent Santa includes building and increasing these skills. And finally, you need a solid repertoire of Santa performance lore from which you can build any performance with any audience.

There are three broad skill sets to hone and polish.

Visual Performance: How you appear, situational awareness, and controlling your environment.

Physical Performance: Body language, physicality, gestures, characterization, and physical interaction.

Vocal Performance: The art of being heard, voice projection, timbre, speaking versus orating, the power of suggestion.

Visual Performance

As Santa, the moment you arrive in full kit, in public, you are on stage. You are watched, photographed, and sought after. You are personally responsible for the image you project. And while you have some control over your image, you will not always have control over every scenario or circumstance. Part of building a rock-solid persona—creating and keeping the most believable Santa performance possible—includes thorough preparation and building a set of pre-performance routines.

Your performance preparation includes far more than just acquiring and maintaining great costuming. The actual performance itself requires preparation, even when you are only preparing for a fifteen-minute performance.

Exercise Assignment: Take an afternoon at home to practice assembling and getting ready to leave for a gig. Start with a complete written check-list of all the items you need to look your best for a Santa engagement. Set a timer and complete all the steps in your kit preparation. Ensure that the fur trim on your outfit has been fluffed, your clothes have been brushed, your boots and brass are polished, your face, beard, and hair are carefully groomed. Pack any cool vest inserts, your personal snacks or drinks, and an emergency change of clothing. Assemble a full supply of candy canes. Check for jingle bells, a Santa bag for gifts, or any props used on the assignment. Complete any make-up application needed, brush your teeth and freshen your breath. See that all your bags are neatly packed, everything has been neatly packed in your car. Stop the timer.

How long did that assignment take? An hour? Longer? Did the time to complete every step from start to finish surprise you? Were there any items missing from your checklist?

It is imperative that you know how long it takes to have your cool vest inserts frozen, the time it takes to reassemble your props or candy cane supplies, and a snack bag for your own food and drinks. Your checklist is important, even when you have a rhythm and you've been doing this for years. Some days, that checklist will save you from your own exhaustion or the well-meaning "help" of someone who thought they would just "move this bag for you." Your preparation time must be part of your calculation for your performance schedules.

One main reason you might not look your best is simply that you were rushed. Preparation pays for itself. Your travel time is affected by the type of traffic congestion or weather patterns (or both!) for your neighborhoods. Any modern computer mapping program might give you accurate estimates for the current conditions, but there are always new traffic accidents or worsening weather conditions that could hit while en route. The mark of a professional includes the performer who always shows up on time (which really means shows up early), nails the performance, and most importantly, makes it look effortless and easy, every time.

Handy Santa True Tip: Use your preparation time to practice. Do vocal exercises in the shower, where the humidity and heat help relax your vocal cords and open your sinuses. Print the words to "The Night Before Christmas" and tape them to the wall or mirror. Rehearse the lines while you dry your hair and complete your final-looks in the mirror.

Now that you have a solid routine to get ready, the next key to your visual performance is the crucial moment when you arrive on-site. Before you step out of any vehicle or approach the door, build a self-inspection routine. Two tools are invaluable: Reflective surfaces and a smart phone.

Start with a visual scan. Practice a thorough review from head to foot. Pull your jacket down completely in the back, adjust your waist band, and check the alignment of your belt buckle. Ensure that your hat pin is exactly where it should be. Check your cuffs and gloves, make certain they are tugged into position. Use the mirror you stored in your Santa prep kit. Use the mirror in your car. Use the windows on your car or other cars in the area. Check your reflection in a mall window. Use the camera on your phone to snap photos or even a short video to double-check that everything is in place.

Most importantly, be confident in your image. This confidence you carry helps others believe in you.

<u>Visual imagery is important</u>. One of the most lasting legacies you will leave is one of the strangest in modern society.

You will be that anonymous Santa on the shelf in the picture of the kids. Decades later, those kids will be grown. And although no one may ever know your name (real or Santa name), one look at that picture will tell you if that Santa and photographer were on their game. This is part of your legacy, your contribution to the tradition of Santa.

Exercise Assignment: Before you go out on assignment or for any performances, get together with some trusted friends and a decent camera. Try staging your own Santa photo shoot. Recreate some of the most popular Santa photo poses. Check online before the shoot to make a list of typical images. Take some pictures with friends standing off to one side, standing behind Santa's chair, with someone on Santa's knee. Use a large stuffed animal to recreate holding a small child in your lap. Lean into a whispered conversation. Hold a small baby (doll). Pose with a friend as they try to take a selfie with their camera.

Now look at these test photos critically. How does your costume look? How is your posture? Are the buttons on your jacket aligned neatly? Is your belt buckle centered properly? Is any part of your costume bunching oddly? How does the drape of the fabric work in different poses? How do your knees and boots look in different poses? Is it time to consult with your costumer, seamstress, or tailor to fix the fit of your coat or pants? Sometimes a small repair makes all the difference between schlumpy and stylish. Check your beard in the photos: How's the color in the photos with or without a flash? Do you have any circles under your eyes?

Has your beard shifted by rubbing against your fur collar? Is there glare on your glasses? Any fixes from these practice photo sessions will go into your preparation checklist.

When evaluating your practice photos or even reflecting on your professional gig images, there are always four key focuses.

1. **Your Smile**. Santa needs to smile, not just with his mouth, but with his cheeks and eyes as well. Ask your photographer to remind you, just in case. Your photographer needs to think "Smile and Hands" before every picture. And now, with everyone carrying a camera in their phones, when you see a hand come up to take a photo, be ready with your complete Santa smile.

   Your Posture. Santa performances can be grueling and long. You might feel like a glorified seat cushion. Your posture will convey energy both to you and in the pictures. Adjust yourself so that nothing is binding. Move slightly forward so that you have both feet on the ground and your back is straight. Make certain that you are not shallow breathing. Make it a habit to stand up fairly regularly to keep the blood flowing and your breathe going. Roll your shoulders and shake it out. Take that moment to adjust your jacket and move. These moments are good chances to wave, say hi, and get a bit of bounce back into your step. Take these moments to hydrate, as well. Hydration is very important, especially to someone wearing a very warm suit.

   Your Santa Pose Repertoire. (See? Performance!) Every Santa is different, but we all have certain looks that we pull off well. Try different smiles: the surprised Santa face, the laughing super- jolly look with head thrown back (such as in

Ed Taylor's photos), the regal Santa face, the mischievous playful Santa face with a raised eyebrow, looking over your glasses, wagging your finger in jest. Build a variety of favorite looks. Some will develop over time. Your goal is to be able to give a variety of expressions and poses quickly, while not looking too staged. Make a list.

Placement and Eye-line. It is very important to look at your hand placement. We want both hands obvious in the picture wherever possible. Go online and look at photos of A-list Santas and try to emulate them. Avoid having hands in weird positions, in or near your crotch, or just out of view but at unusual angles. It can be hard to tell what works best, so talk to your photographer. Likewise, when very busty ladies are in your lap, be certain that your face and head are angled so that you are looking up into the camera, not making you look awkward. This happens especially if you smile up at their face while they are on your knee. Try to lean back a bit and twist your torso away, tilting your eyes to look over your glasses. Seriously, one badly posed photo can float around the internet for a very long time. Awareness is critical.

Remember that it is difficult to know how you look until you examine the photos. Some of your smiles might make you appear to squint, especially depending on the height of the chair or the camera height. Some photos may look better if your head was tilted the other way. You might want to experiment with the twist of your torso.

Every time you work with a photographer, try some test shots at the beginning. Take a look and get some feedback. After a group of photos, ask your photographer to look at them critically, and ask if you can see them yourself. As needed, reset your posture and poses before the next batch. If you perform a home visit, always ask if they can send copies of photos to you. This helps you keep track of how you are doing. And, with their permission, you can collect some nice photos to help you with your Santa marketing.

Knowing how to take good Santa photos and how to orchestrate good photo placement is very important, especially in scenarios where you are visiting a hospital or a private home. The experienced Santa knows when to step in with some careful suggestions. Most people have cameras with them and they do not always know where to stand to take good photos or how to set the shot so that Santa and friends look well framed. This is where the photo-experienced Santa comes in. Let's look at an example.

"Ho-ho-ho! Momma Jackson, why don't we take one of those sturdy, straight-back dining room chairs right there and put that green plaid throw over it? Shall we move Santa away from the fire and sit over by the Christmas tree, away from all that reflective glass? This way you won't have flashes bouncing back in the photos. Tim and Tina, could we move some these presents over here? Maybe we can have the teens stand on either side of me, and we could put Fluffy here on the footstool right next to me?

Could we could put little Nellie in my lap for the photos? Mrs. Jackson, what if you stand right there? And after you get some good wide shots, would you like to step in to get some close-ups, too? How does that sound? Shall we turn on this lamp? Ho! Excellent! Now everyone will see what a beautiful tree you have!"

Months later when that client comes back to you and says, "We took the most amazing photos of you!" then you can nod and smile and say, "Amazing! You have a great eye! I hope you shared them!"

You will also note that in this example, Santa did the following:

Phrased everything as a question.

Got away from the roaring fireplace, to avoid being a sweaty mess.

Arranged proper seating, so as to not to be in the Santa-eating chair.

Distanced everyone from inadvertent reflections.

Made it all look pretty.

Arranged it so the teens could stand alongside him, and the dog was not on his suit.

Involved everyone.

Turned on an extra lamp, so there was more ambient lighting so the auto-focus would work.

Santa Sneaky, eh? This is a subtle part of controlling the Visual image you want to project, but an important one. Photographs are part of your visual performance. And while we are discussing performing photographs....

Video cameras are now part of most smart phones and most digitals cameras, whether point-and-shoot or DSLR cameras. If you have a situation in which you are being videotaped by many people at the same time, make certain your energy is up. And if you like, nod toward the camera, as if acknowledging it. But your primary focus remains being genuine to the people you are in direction interaction with. Occasionally, you will run into people who want to direct you or videotape every last bit. It adds a different dynamic to the situation. This video could be up on YouTube very quickly. So always be polite and carefully stay in character. If you focus on creating a relationship with the people around you, it will look genuine on camera. And it is okay to say something like, "Did you get enough video? I want to make sure you get a chance to relax, too! Why don't we turn off the cameras for a bit while I get situated, and I will remind you when to turn the cameras back on? Wonderful!"

Speaking of cameras, video technology has grown. Now people can easily pull up Skype or video messaging software and ask you to record a message or talk to someone via a video link. Be careful. This is where Santa's all-knowing omniscience can fail you. Suddenly you are talking to a little girl who wants to discuss "Mipsy" (their elf on the shelf) and you have no clue. What about her dog? Her sister? and so on. So if you agree to speak by video, set some conditions engage the other person as your co-conspirator. Find out the following and set the rules.

"I would be delighted! But I can only do this for a short time, I'm afraid. Let me say hi to these folks over here, while you get the video ready. And what can you tell me about the following? Tell me about your relationship, who we will we be talking to, how old are they, have they been good? Is there anything they could improve on, did they do anything really well this year? Is there an Elf on the Shelf in their family, and if so what is its name? Have they sent Santa an e-mail or letter this year? And is there anything else special I should know?"

Note that the Santa is not sitting there while the person is trying to lock on their Wi-Fi, get the app going, or clean their lenses. Suddenly they realize that you, as a Santa performer, are giving them something of value. Then the video recording can be shaped something like this.

X is right here and they wanted me to say hi! I am delighted to see you.

Are you excited about Christmas? Santa is so excited about Christmas, it's my favorite time of year!

_____ have you been a good boy or girl? You have? Wonderful, keep up the good work!

Well, I will be delivering a special present for you soon on Christmas. And don't forget my cookies and milk, and don't forget, my reindeer love carrots!

X, thank you for letting me talk to them. And, MERRY CHRISTMAS!

If the people on the other side of the phone want to keep it going, you can tell them that Santa has to take care of things where you are. They can send you an e-mail or a letter, with their parents help, of course.

Your goal is to delight the person taking the video, and the amaze the recipients. Make certain you hand them a card at the end of it.

Visual performance is also part of live performance, not just for the cameras. One of the most important things you can do as a pro-Santa is gain situational awareness and the ability to control your environment. Here are some key things to remember and some examples.

1. **You ARE the Pro Santa**. You are responsible for how you want to be seen. And while the client may have some experience, you are usually the most experienced Santa in the room. *"Hello Mary, I just happened to notice your pets are getting really excited. Could we have them put in another room for right now? I don't want to scare them."*

Establish your expertise. By taking charge, you are helping the client get the best experience out of what they are paying for. *"Hi Mike, this looks amazingly wonderful! You look like the person in charge, and as this is not Santa's first sleigh-ride, I just wanted to ask you a question or two. I see tables full of sweets and video games but not very many adults.*

We will need adults to supervise the kids. Santa is not a baby-sitter and I cannot take photos with them in my lap without the parents being in the room with us. Any thoughts?" In the above statement Santa has done three things. He's established his concerns, made the person he's talking to feel in charge, and done it in the form of a question so it is not threatening. By stepping up and asking questions, Santa has just prevented a screaming three-ring circus, because the parents indeed had planned on going into another room for drinks. It happens.

You cannot control everything. Sometimes you just have to roll with it. But here's a tip you can use from improvisation classes in theater. They use a rule called "Go for the agreement." This means that if someone hands you an imaginary frog, your character does not say, "No, it isn't. It's an apple." That kills the scene and the momentum. In improv, you say *"Yes! And..."* In this case the performer keeps it rolling by saying, *"Yes, a frog! Mortimer, you singing dancing frog you, how have you been?"*

Santa is playful and fun. And people want a chance to have fun. Even adults! Let's say for some reason, they have parked you and your Santa chair right next to the door to the restaurant kitchen. There's no way for you to get them to move you in the time allotted. Staff fly in and out, and it's really awkward. Ignoring it will be hard. So a creative Santa can ask all the kids and folks to be his co-conspirators. You could say, "Every time one of them comes through, I want you to turn your head and say Merry Christmas!

And then turn back to me, right away!" A few fun "Merry Christmases" later, the disruption has been acknowledged and becomes second hand.

Pretty soon all the wait-staff are in on it, and everyone in the place is hearing a regular, "Merry Christmas" from the corner.

Santa is strongest when he is genuine and fun. So make the best of strange situations. Here are some places where your Visual performance is going to get noticed.

Grand Entrances. When Santa comes into a room, he comes *into* a room. Ask your escort what is ahead of you. You might hand them your bags and arrange your jacket and parade coat. Or you could hand them your jingle bells while you enter slowly—large and in charge. After you've made eye contact with everyone and thanked them for inviting you, then go around and shake hands with everyone while you re-introduce yourself.

"Hello! (shake-shake) My name is Santa, pleased to meet you!"

Why do both? Two good reasons. First, when you first come in, your visual image is striking. You worked hard on your image and you want folks to get an eyeful. Secondly, the up-close and personal is establishing the social contract in which we agree that I am Santa Claus. The psychology of that moment is wonderful, if a bit hidden, because deep down, a tiny part of them in the back of their head is asking, "OMG, what if this *is the real Santa*? I am shaking hands with *SANTA!*" This adds excitement to the moment.

Smaller Entrances. If you are dealing with little ones in a family setting, you may want to dial it back. Shake hands with the adults.

And if you have one kid who rushes to you, go down to a knee (if you can) and pull them in for a hug. Afterwards, ask them to take you by the hand and lead you into the room. *"Can you show me your Christmas Tree?"* Also, bring down the volume. And when you are talking to the client before you show up, make certain that any excitable animals are going to be kept locked up for the duration.

Parades and Public Events. If you are moving, be very aware of where your coat, hat, and any accessories are going to be. If you are riding on something, place yourself where you can brace yourself and where people can get an unobstructed view of you. Be prepared for sudden stops or wind. Gestures should be all upper body and large. If possible, get a sound system with a head-set microphone and light colored wind-screen. Make certain the speakers are not immediately behind you, to avoid feedback. Try to find out what the local populations are (for instance, Spanish or Danish) and learn how to say Merry Christmas in those languages.

Public Areas or On Streets. First, never let Santa be a traffic hazard. Be especially carefully around kids or folks who might rush to you. You never want to accidentally endanger someone, so situational awareness is critical. If possible, in public, always have an assigned handler (it could be an Elf, a friend, a security person). Survey your area.

If you are performing in the round (audience on all sides), make certain that people are not going to accidentally flip over benches, chains, or fences. If the ground is muddy or slippery, you might be fine (since Santa is wearing boots) but others might not be. So, please be aware for your audience.

Good Lighting. Your goal is to get a medium level of overall lighting, with a bit of back light and some good front lighting. Too bright can make your face and beard look washed out. Too dark, and many cameras won't be able to autofocus, and your costume will look dark and muddy (especially if it's a plush burgundy). Pay attention to audio as well. Avoid areas with a heavy background noise, or super hard reflective surfaces (which are problematic for both light and audio bounce back). Areas with natural greenery, warm tones, wood, or rocks look good in photos.

Handy Santa True Tip: If you are ever need a quick generic background for photos or headshots, find a wall full of healthy ivy. It's a natural backdrop. Likewise, a stand of pine trees with nothing else obvious in the background can be very Christmas-y!

If you are working in a mall or shopping center, be aware that in a busy place, you will get stopped for "just one photo." This can then turn into a hundred, and you will make a snail's pace to where you are going. (Ask any Mall Santa about this.) That's why Mall Santas are often escorted by elves or security.

But often times, you've just shown up to a gig, solo, and you are trying to get to where you need to be. This is the time to break out the industrial strength Jolly and just keep moving while saying, *"Merry Christmas! Why thank you! Yes, let's take pictures, I'm headed to my chair!"* Don't do this loudly, just conversationally.

Other visual moments. Santa is iconic. So if Santa participates in photo bombs when people are not expecting it, this can be a ton of fun and a great way to be noticed, especially when you don't seem to have many folks visiting you in the chair. Just be prepared to do more traditional photos after you do. Likewise, if you run into authority figures, have an extra Santa hat handy or pose for a "back to back" photo. For smaller visual moments, when someone spies you getting in or out of your car, just give them a wink and the finger on the lips—it's a secret!

If you want more ideas, go online and search "Santa Claus News" or "Real Santa Claus Photos," then look through the images. As you page through the search results, look closely at the pictures of Santas with problems: Wrinkled costumes, bad posture, odd lighting, or strange beards. Now look through the photos again for the successful Santa images: Great eyes, good posture, and other things stand out. Look for "dynamic" images that look alive and "genuine" contact between Santa and the camera or Santa and other people.

Your goal is to always appear solid and excellent. You will want to use your visual templates—your poses, ability to work with your environment, your facial expressions—with ease and consistency.

Physical Performance

Your physical performance includes body language, physicality, gestures and characterization, and your complete physical interaction.

As mentioned earlier, Santa is an iconic character. Everyone has an idea of how Santa should look, act, and behave. And over the years, especially through advertising, we have seen Santa do everything from skateboarding to cartwheels. But most people dismiss that as "Hollywood."

But let's take a moment to think about the lore. Santa is magical. His delivery night is beyond human capability. He must be powerful, if only because he drives a sleigh and carries a big bag over his shoulder. He's tough enough to live at the North pole, devour metric tons of milk and cookies, and run the biggest toy company in the world. So our character can range from an older obese man in his 60's to a magical being capable of almost anything. But the truth is, we are mere mortals who portray him, and we often do not have amazing capabilities. Furthermore, when Santa seems to have typical human frailties like a bad back, bum knee, gas, or a cold, it tends to humanize him and takes some of the magic away from our portrayal. But there are ways we can use our physicality to portray him in ways to help build belief and magic.

Exercise Assignment: One key method for getting into the skin of a character is always give your character something specific to do. Let's take a character from a fairy tale, the Big Bad Wolf. Take a few moments and try some exercises around the house. How does the Big Bad Wolf brush his teeth? How does he eat a sandwich? How does he worry about something? How does he react to a big bill in the mail? Try several tasks, use your imagination, and have fun.

Notice anything about how you expressed yourself? Was your big, bad wolf low and growly? Was he more of a slick-zoot suit kind of guy? Or was he harried and a hen-pecked sort of bad guy? Were his actions tight and focused, or relaxed and loose? Was he continually ready to pounce or just kind of annoyed?

In theater and in storytelling, characters often use a key gesture or phrase. By playing with our characters, we discover mannerisms, vocal expressions, and physical traits. This can be a tool for you, too! Admittedly, if you are Santa for ten hours a day in a mall, the lines between your expressions and those of the Santa are going to get pretty blurry. But say you were doing a home visit, a corporate event, or an audition. Being able to call up that key gesture or phrase will help you lock into your character and help you bring him to life. Even if you yourself are not having a good day, or you find yourself a bit tired or nervous, knowing how to get "in the skin" of your character can be really helpful. Your key gesture could be as simple as hooking your thumbs in your belt, leaning back, and chuckling. Or perhaps you sing the opening of Rudolph the Red Nose Reindeer.

Here are some other tips on physical performance.

1. **Think from your audience's point of view**. The size and scope of your physical gestures will vary depending on where you are and what you are doing. If you are in a Parade, you want your gestures to be broad and smooth. If you are at a home visit, move your gestures from the center of your torso out, and be gentle if you have many small children about. If you get a chance to experiment, sit down with someone else playing the role of Santa and look up. What do you see? How will children see you? If you are in a public venue, will only the front ranks be able to see you? Is there anything you can do about that?

2. **Body Language**. When you search for images of Santa on the internet, it's easy to see both good and bad body language. One of the key problems is slumping. Often the chairs provided for Santa are too deep. Very imperceptibly, when we wear a hat, beard, and/or glasses, our heads tend to come down and our shoulders to roll

forward. Teach yourself to monitor your posture on a regular basis.

When seated, Santa should be in an "open" position: feet and legs apart, leaning slightly forward, head tilted, and hands relaxed.

Learn to read your audience: Are their arms crossed? Do you see hand clenching or wringing, or possibly foot tapping? Learning to read your audience can help you target the right performance at the right time.

Keep in mind that different cultures have different styles. In some cultures, touching is very common whereas in others, touching is reserved for specific relationships.

Micro-expressions. Did you know that we all have tiny expressions as well as body language that convey our feelings? If you are exasperated and your smile is forced, you will have a tiny expression flit across your face. People are quick to pick up on that, even if it's subliminal. Many Santas are pretty good at picking up on that, too.

Take some time to do some people watching. Notice how people show confidence and playfulness, and attentiveness. While standing, a confident person has feet firmly planted, shoulder width apart, shoulders are back, head is still, arms are held lightly to the front. No fidgeting and movements are steady. Also, talk a bit slower and take good-sized strides, survey your domain. Now, look at playfulness, engagement, and attentiveness. What do you see?

Learn to make sincere eye contact. Also learn where eye contact can come off as aggressive.

Body Language. Santa is one of the few roles in today's culture where touching still happens. Folks sit in laps and give hugs. Take advantage of this (but not in a creepy way). Shake hands and introduce yourself. This creates a "buy-in" and closes the physical space. Santa can pat someone on the back during a laugh, take both of someone's hands in theirs as a gesture of sincerity. Children often times want hugs. Learn how to do this with one leg forward when they come flying in, and offer a warm one-handed hug or pat.

There is so much to learn about physical performance and about reading other people's body language and micro-expressions, you would be amazed. Watch the best actors: they can create a character with a prop, several words, and just a few actions. It's amazing. But remember, from the moment you were born, you've been studying other people. You are much better than you know at picking out subtle things. You can you use this to your Santa advantage.

Vocal Performance

Your vocal performance includes volume, projection, tone, pitch, enunciation, diction, among other details.

What does Santa sound like? What *does* Santa sound like? Ask yourself. Go ahead, we'll wait. You might say something like, "Jolly, baritone, bass, rumbly."

Human beings learn in a variety of ways, whether that's visually, aurally, kinetically, or a combination of these methods. Chances are, at some point in your life, you keyed in on a Santa that just made the moment for you. And forever more, Santa, the real Santa, sounds like that memory to you. Often times, we use movie memories that come to us from Hollywood. Some of the most famous Hollywood Santas had very distinctive voices. Those voices came to them by the way of years of acting or performance training.

When we hear the gruff growl of Ed Asner, the snarky tones of Tim Allen, the various complex tones of Tom Hanks, or the cultured voices of Richard Attenborough or Edmund Gwenn, we are listening to some of the best of the best.

And you may need to forgive folks if they want you to be just as good as a trained actor who also had a host of audio technicians, mixers, and sound men plus some great writers behind them.

Here's the good news: As Santa, we create our own little reality. Make a good first impression, get buy-in from your audience and, voila, that other memory gets pushed to the back.

Santa is at first a visual figure. He's very striking and brightly colored. But then, as soon as he comes in and makes a grand figure, we find ourselves anticipating the hearty "ho-ho-ho!" At the end of the evening, Santa wraps up with a great big, "Meeerrrry Christmas and to all a good night!" It would be very odd if he sounded like Daffy Duck. A great vocal performance is the jelly to our peanut butter, the cheese to the cracker. Things like this help us nail our recreation of Santa. And vocal ability takes consistent, ongoing PRACTICE.

First, let's be clear: Everyone has a natural voice range. This range can be expanded with training. Training also improves volume, projection, timbre, and singing on key. Your voice is created by a set of muscles and attributes.

Very few people are born with a voice like Patrick Stewart (Jean-Luc Picard), who could read the side of a cereal box and people would pay him good money to do so. He is also a classically trained Shakespearean actor, emphasis on the word "trained."

Our goal as Santa is to give our natural abilities a little extra oomph. Even if you have a high pitched voice, or perhaps it seems raspy, or you have an accent—your natural voice is fine. If you continue to work on speaking and vocal technique, it will pay off big time down the road.

Here are some specific things you can work on to improve your vocal performance.

1. **Be Prepared and Practice**. Why? Because uncertainty brings stress and your audience can pick up on it. Stress reduces your vocal capability. Confidence in your material helps you relax. And people pick up on confidence, too!

2. **Breathing**. There are any number of breathing exercises that can help you develop greater volume, projection, and airflow. Increased airflow helps your stamina. If you are trapped completing a 20-minute performance in a noisy room for a large audience, vocal stamina really pays off. Breath is life. Your goal is to let your breath always come free and easy, with no tightness.

3. **Flexibility**. You want to stay loose during your performances. Before you perform, always loosen up for a bit beforehand. Use a quick set of both physical and vocal exercises to warm up—it will really help in the long run.

4. **Position and Posture**. How you are standing or sitting can make a world of difference. One of the nice things about being Santa is that we can let our bellies out, taking advantage of our natural diaphragm. Practice your best standing and sitting vocal positions.

5. **Pacing**. When we are nervous, full of energy, or stressed, we tend to speed up. This then affects your natural tone, musical key, and how fast you complete your performance. When you practice, record your rehearsals.

Try a variety of speeds. If you typically perform, "The Night Before Christmas," try it fast, medium, and slow. Time yourself. Later in performance, if you know that you only have a specific time limit, you'll already know which speed to use for your recitation, story, or song.

6. **Sincerity**. If you sound too forced, staged, or pompous, you will lose your audience. Part of the key is making great eye contact and speaking to a person, genuinely. Warm tones work best in closer environments like home visits. Know what you want to say and care about it.

7. **Pitch**. There are a variety of websites and tools you can use to make certain are you are singing in key. Santa can carry a pitch pipe or have a pitch pipe app on his smart phone, very easily. When we sing, we can be either sharp or flat on a specific note. Sometimes our own ears betray us: We might think we are on pitch when we are not. Seek out friends or family that have musical training or look for a vocal coach or choir director who can help you evaluate your skills.

8. **Inflection, Emphasis, and Rhythm**. Take for instance the verse for "5 Golden Rings" in the "Twelve Days of Christmas." Everyone belts out, *"Fiiiiiiiiiiivvvveee Gooooooolden Riiinnnnggss."* If we did that same emphasis for, "Threeeeee Frrrreeeeennnchhh Heeeeennnns," it would sound rather odd. Whether we are singing, storytelling, or doing a reading, we have a variety of speeds, rhythms, and emphasis points we can use. See the exercise, "Twas the Night before Christmas."

9. **Volume and Projection**. Volume is a physical measurement of how loud we are. Loudness is also a relative term. If you are yelling in a loud factory, it may not even be noticed. Knowing how to gauge your volume

in various environments is a learned skill. Voice projection is the strength and quality of the voice, paired with an ability to be heard clearly. A person who has trained at projecting their voice uses less energy and can be heard more clearly. The quality of their voice is more resonant and robust. Voice projection requires clear breathing and a good stance, as well as an understanding on how our vocal apparatus works. You may need to seek out a trained vocal professional for assistance with projection.

10. **Articulate**. Just like warming up before doing physical work, you can warm up with your vocals before you perform. Try some tongue twisters, singing scales, or rehearsing some pieces that are challenging. Articulation is especially important if your voice is naturally in a low register. If you have a strong accent, specific speech issues such as stutter, or if you have dental issues, doing a few vocal articulation exercises as a warm up is an excellent idea.

Try recording yourself. Have someone help you listen critically, to see if you have any verbal issues that you might want to address.

11. **Exercise Assignment**: There are many verbal or articulation exercises available on the internet. Try this tongue-twister for the letter B. "Betty bought a bit of butter, but she found the butter bitter, so Betty bought a bit of better butter to make the bitter butter better."

How did the tongue twister work? What other practice phrases make you focus on the consonants and vowels in your speech?

12. **Exercise Assignment**: Try reading "Twas The Night Before Christmas" through, as basically as possible. Now

do it again faster. Then do it again, but this time shake it up a bit. Emphasize some lines but not others. Do some as whispers and some really loud. Then do it again in character, not just Santa, but as a little kid, or a sleepy adult, or with an accent. Have fun with it. Now, take all those experiments, and hold the book to your side and present the story while pointing to the pictures. Try to maintain as much eye contact with your (imaginary) audience as possible.

Which reading had the most meaning to you? What did you discover that seemed like a new, great idea? Which reading gave you the most trouble? Which seemed the easiest?

13.   **Handy Santa True Tip**: You can videotape yourself and then give yourself feedback. Also, take some copies of songs that you want to sing with you, and play them in the car just before the gig.

Storytelling Basics

First, consider that we are all storytellers. All of us learn through stories, tell stories, enjoy stories. It is one of the first art forms and has had a profound effect on humanity. Some of humanities greatest influencers were storytellers: Abraham Lincoln, Mark Twain, Jesus Christ, Buddha, the list goes on and on. Anyone can tell a story.

Learning to be a master storyteller can take a lifetime. We can't cover everything, but we can explore some questions and suggestions about the art that encompasses myth, folklore, legend, fairy-tales, and tall tales,

Stories and Santa. If there is one character in modern Western media that is a better example of the power of storytelling than Santa, I am hard put a name to it.

Christmas (outside of religious connotations) is a huge cultural movement and industry in Western society. Anyone who knows about the history of Santa Claus and his various elements—from St. Nicholas of Myra of Turkey to the Yule influences, to cultural influences from the Norse, Celtic, and Anglo-Saxons—know that Santa is an amalgamation of folklore, myth, religion, marketing, and creative advertising. Not only is the story of Santa one that we still share and celebrate every year, it is ongoing, changing, and evolving. And every professional Santa is bringing those stories to life, which is pretty amazing. If we look at the societal role of Santa, his role in a very traditional sense could be called shamanic or priestly. He is magical and identified by his clothing, hair style, and annual ride. We trust little children to him, he has a judging role, and he lives outside the bounds of normal society.

In nearly all early cultures, that quasi-religious role was filled by people who understood the power of story. That story could entertain but also create truth, understanding, and cross cultural boundaries. So it should be no surprise that our modern Santas should be one of the few roles where it's okay for Santa to come in and share some stories.

At this point, let me make a distinction. There are all sorts of stories, storytellers, and storytelling techniques and story props. But for our purposes, let's define storytelling as a story that we would tell without the use of book or reading something. If you are reading a story from a book, you are doing a recitation or a reading. (This *can* be entertaining, but **is not** *storytelling* per se.)

So what do we mean by storytelling?

Storytelling happens when we share a story that has a beginning, middle, and end. It is told directly to the audience and direct eye contact is made. While Santa can be telling a story about his life and events, he is not an actor but he is relating something.

Why tell stories? For lots of good reasons!

Santa lives because of stories.

If you are a great storyteller, you can captivate audiences and share a skill that we don't get enough of these days.

You can create your own stories, unique to you, tailored for your audiences.

Stories pack pretty easily.

A good storyteller does not need a lot expensive props, instruments, etc. You can sit down, and ask, "Do you want to hear a story from Santa?"

Storytelling is good for kids. Science has shown that the ability to follow oral narrative and actively visualize it is great for cognition among a host of other skills.

To paraphrase Albert Einstein, "If you want your children to be to be intelligent, tell them fairy tales. If you want them to be more intelligent, tell them more fairytales."

The messages you share in your stories can not only strengthen people's belief in the values of Christmas Spirit, but a story is a shared journey that everyone, young or old, can go on.

Learn to be a good storyteller and you might find you have saleable skills throughout the year! One of the great things about being a storyteller, there is no mandatory retirement age. And having a long white beard is not such a bad thing! Storytelling is an amazing tool for communicating effectively, and it can be used in a variety of ways. Storytelling is important to public speaking, sales, grief counseling, working with at risk kids—you name it. [For more on storytelling, check out the National Storytelling Networks, A Beginners Guide to Storytelling (a handy little book).]

First, how do we choose a story?

Listen. Believe it or not, spoken word is still being done. You can go to storytelling events, watch storytellers online on YouTube, and attend storytelling events. It's considered bad form to completely copy another teller's stories without permission. But most traditional stories have multiple variants. Look for other versions and create something that resonates with you. You can also perform personal stories from your life and stories you created.

Read. There are hundreds of traditional stories and created stories out there. Be careful when looking at something that has a Newbury or Caldecott award, or something from Disney. Make certain when you perform that you make it your own. If you perform something that is part of a trademark, you could have issues. If you are looking for traditional stories, August House lists many good resources at http://www.augusthouse.com/ Try searching the Internet for "traditional folk tales." You will find a variety on the web.

Evaluate. Every story has pluses and minuses. It has a "Most important thing" (often times a message), plus the characters and plot. Every audience and event is different. Picking the right story, for the right time and place, takes practice. Generally, the younger the audience, you want to make it more interactive (like call and response), less scary, and maybe more funny. Older audiences enjoy more dramatic, insightful, clever stories. But the great thing is that as your repertoire grows, your ability to reach out to your audiences will, too.

Grow. As you tell your stories, you will discover things that audiences laugh at or the places where you seem to lose them. Some sound effects and gestures work or don't.

Your story will talk to you and change as you tell it. Plus your skills as a storyteller will shift as you develop your voice and style. How can you grow as a storyteller? Always look for new stories, new opportunities to see other tellers, and new chances to tell to new audiences.

Get to know your story. Most stories have something in common: Plot, struggle, goal, and resolution. Learn the story sequences. Look into what's called "the Aristotelian Theme." There are a variety of ways to map out your outline. Try working on a storyboard or a traditional outline. Spend time with each of your characters. Some characters are very one-dimensional. Others have very specific voices or mannerisms. It really helps to know their key gesture or phrase. Doug Lipman, storytelling coach extraordinaire, speaks about the concept of "MIT, or Most Important Thing." The MIT is usually the thing that drew your interest in the story in the first place, the thing that for you drives the story. Knowing your MIT really helps. Many stories also emphasize a message. Rudolph the Red Nosed Reindeer has strong message—or several. What do you think that message is?

Know your audience. This is just as important to a Santa as well as a Storyteller. When we do performances, three things can really help you.

1. **Do your homework**. Find out everything you can about your clients and audience. Your best source of information is the person who hired you.

2. **Interview them to learn as much as possible**: your audience members' ages, what have the people have been up to, what they are expecting, other things that they have done—the whole "who-what-where-when-why-how" comes in handy. Let them know that the better they inform you, the better you can tailor your performance.

3. **Research**. You can do some research on-line and by networking with others who have worked with them.

4. **Arrive early and investigate**. On-site, it's always a good idea to get there early and chat folks up. Of course, as Santa, you have to stay in character, but making friends and asking questions can be really helpful. In some cases, you can always do a little early research off the clock as a non-Santa person.

5. **Using your body and voice.** As a performer and as a storyteller, your primary tools remain your body and your voice. Everyone has some experience getting attention from an audience. Then you can study further to make using your body and voice a learned art. Add to this the presence of Santa. When this is done with an eye towards appropriateness, it can be really effective.

Imagine Santa telling the story of the wolf in Little Red Riding Hood (or some type of Christmas variant). When Santa says something in falsetto with a bonnet tied under his nose, the little kids will be rolling in the aisles with laughter. Remember, Santa is toymaker-in-chief and must have a playful heart, to know what toys will work best.

Santa can be many characters. When he performs as a character, the fact that he is Santa takes his appearance to the back for that period of time. Personal stories and stories you create yourself can also have voices, gestures, and characterizations.

Using costumes, props, and instruments. In the Little Red Riding Hood example, your "costume" might just be a bonnet. Or maybe you use a set of goofy reindeer horns. In some Santa-specific stories, one of the new items many Santas carrying is the "Magic Key" which allows Santa to get into places that don't have chimneys.

If Santa lost the key or had it swiped, you could have the makings of story that fits nicely into the story you can tell. Instruments can be great fun, and music fits hand and glove into storytelling. For inspiration, look to the folk music and comedian communities.

How do I get started as a Storytelling Santa? First of all, think of yourself as a Storyteller. There are many storytelling organizations with events and festivals. Since Santa works with children so frequently, I would recommend trying some stories on some friendly groups, children of friends, or maybe someone's grandkids. Once you have a few practice audiences and stories under your belt, find a friend who knows something about performance. They can help you evaluate what works and what does not. Then practice some more.

How does this effect what I offer, and how do I pitch this to my clients? Before you offer it as an option, make certain you feel comfortable doing it.

Have a variety of stories to offer and know exactly how long they run. Many people don't know what a storyteller does. *"Oh, you're a Storyteller... So, you read books to kids, right?"* I hear that comment from time to time. So you may need to explain what you do and give them a very brief synopsis, a couple of sentences should do. The main advantage that being a storytelling Santa gives you is content. You can add this to your list of performance options and delight audiences, and give longer performances for your clients.

A word about Storytelling Etiquette, some advice:

Make certain you do your best to avoid going over time.

Your audience comes first. Don't bore them and always leave them wanting more.

Try to make certain your story fits the right type of audience.

Don't duplicate stories you've heard from others, without getting permission first.

Watch out for copyrighted stories. If you make money doing something that a company owns, that could be a problem.

Do your best to always improve your art.

Help other storytellers when you can.

Your stories and storytelling have value. Don't undersell yourself.

Singing for Santas

This may be more familiar ground, since most Santas have lead people in "Rudolph the Red Nosed Reindeer," "Jingle Bells," and more. But if you want to raise it to another level, let's look at some options and concerns. First, be aware that people in today's culture are often uncomfortable when asked to sing, but kids usually don't have that problem. Children want to participate. Adults can be slow to start or some want to jump right in. In all cases, it usually can't hurt to ask the clients if this is agreeable to them. Then inquire which songs might be most appropriate. Overly religious songs might make some people feel awkward, while "Grandma got run over by a reindeer" might be just a bit too humorous for some crowds.

Handy Santa True Tip: I like to carry a batch of small jingle bells on bands. I hand one to an adult or teen who can help the kids stay on time and then demonstrate. "Everybody ready? *** Jingle Bells, ***Jingle Bells, and so on. The key is to stay high energy, and interactive, and very encouraging.

Do you have training as a singer? There are many ways to get training as a singer. You can join a barbershop quartet, a choir, or find a vocal coach. Or find a school that has music classes. Some organizations like Boy Scouts also encourage singing and are always looking for people to help. If you have friends who do karaoke, they can often point you in the right direction. Plus there are many resources online, including YouTube. Remember that when you perform, you want to make certain you stay on key, know your lyrics, and project at the right volume for the room (soft where appropriate, boisterous and ringing where needed).

Before you start tackling seriously challenging songs like, "Oh Holy Night" in front of an audience, be sure that this is the right audience, and that you can do this song, perfectly on key, every time, and that you've had someone who is a trained singer give you the thumbs up before you take it on the road.

Do you have a repertoire? Songs are like stories. You need the right songs for the right audience. It's generally a good idea to have at least a few very popular and simple secular (non-religious) songs. Practice singing "Rudolph the Red Nosed Reindeer," "Jingle Bells," "Santa Claus is Coming to Town."

If you have some songs in other languages, like "Feliz Navidad" or "Riu, Riu, Chiu," you will win big smiles from an audience that include people who speak that language natively (as long as you do it right).

Common Christmas carols often have some religious elements, which might be good for the right audience. "Silent Night," "Joy to the World," "Tannenbaum (O' Christmas Tree)," "Deck the Halls" are good examples. But if you are performing as Santa for an audience with a higher percentage of Jewish or Indian members, you may need to stick to the secular songs.

For the more sophisticated crowd, traditional Wassailing songs include, "Somerset Wassail," "Here we come a Wassailing," and "We Wish you a Merry Christmas" give you a great opportunity to talk about Christmas traditions of history. Likewise old carols such as the "Sussex Carol," "the Boars Head Carol," and songs like "Gaudete" will impress people who are really into their Christmas lore.

How good is your audience interaction? Use strong vocal projection to make sure everyone can hear you. Before you go on, have a friendly person stationed in the very back to give you a thumbs up or down. When people cannot see you or hear you, that is a real disappointment. But at the other extreme: Don't blast your audience. If you are going to be on microphone, take a class, practice working on microphone, and be very aware of where your speakers are. Remember, amplification does not make your singing voice better – it just makes it louder.

If you are leading a sing-along, you may want to provide some simple handouts that they can keep (coincidentally with your contact info). Not all people can sight-read music, so keep it simple. Remember: Do not charge for the handouts, especially if they contain copyrighted songs. Print the lyrics in larger type, especially if it's going to be outdoors.

The more you interact with your audience, the more they will support the song and join in. You can encourage good voices and enthusiastic people. You can lend your support to folks who are shy, by lowering your voice and joining with them in a non-aggressive manner.

Do you use instruments? Most Santas that play instruments tend to do it very well, and can sing as well. If you are bringing an instrument to a gig, make sure that it is tuned up as soon as you pull it out. It's even better when Santa has an assistant who can do the tuning for the right song and hand it to Santa when ready. Your goal as an instrument-playing Santa is to keep your fiddle time to an absolute minimum.

You likely won't be able play an instrument in gloves. If you are using electronics, the people who are working sound need to know in advance what you need. Also make sure your tuner, if you need one, has fresh batteries and is in working order before the gig. Carry everything you need—for example, if you play guitar, be sure that you have your extra picks, extra strings, Capo, and any other tools.

When there is a festively decorated music stand and instrument stand right out front, this tells folks what is going to happen. If you are performing outdoors, make certain you have sufficient light, and a way to hold any papers down. If you use other cards or aids, be sure there is a place to store them or access them. Also, remember that instruments and props need to be watched and cared for. You don't want someone to step on your five hundred dollar ukulele by accident, because you set it down to take a quick picture.

If you are bringing an instrument, try to find an assistant to take care of your gear and keep it safe from harm. Talk to the event coordinator beforehand, to have them provide a place where you can safely stow it. And learn to do an inventory, when you get ready to leave. If you are providing instruments: jingle bells, kazoos, or what have you, make them cheap, durable, and cleanable, if you intend to reuse them. Remember that little children, under the age of four, should not get jingle bells, due to choking. If you hand out instruments to your audience, hand them to the parents of small children (just to be on the safe side) and let them supervise.

Santas who can sing, tell stories, and play instruments, have a lot of options!

May your performing Santa be excellent, in demand, and may you get that highest of compliments.

"You are the REAL Santa!"

Robert Seutter, aka Santa True and also known as True Thomas the Storyteller, is a professional storyteller and has been storytelling for more than twenty-five years. He has helped create storytelling festivals, and was Director and Chief instigator for a non-profit organization (DreamShapers) dedicated to promoting the folks arts. He is also a published author and a professional "Concierge" Santa, based in Thousand Oaks, CA. He can be reached for workshops, coaching, and performance training, as well as a myriad of storytelling personae, at: robertseutter@gmail.com, santa@santatrue.com, truethomas@sbcglobal.net, and his websites include: truethomas.com, santatrue.com, robertseutter.com, and on Facebook you can find True Thomas the Storyteller, Santa True, and Robert Seutter – Author. Telephone is 818-762-9075, and he's always glad to chat with his fellow performers and help where he can.

*This chapter has been reprinted with permission from Robert Seutter (Santa True), © 2015 TrueCo Publishing.

Note! Since this article was written, Robert Seutter has started a class/school on Performance and being Santa. He has a rather narrow focus on the Santa community and the lack of Performance knowledge New Santa show.

First year or 30 year veteran Santa, Plan to attend a class by Santa True if you can! You will definitely walk away with multiple ideas to incorporate into your presentation! Tell True I sent you!

Songs for singing during a Christmas Visit

Some might be better simply recited as poetry while other could be sung.

We all know Jingle Bells, Rudolph the Red Nosed Reindeer, Santa Claus is Coming to Town and several more but here are a few that might not be familiar to you. All Christmas Carols are of course sung but these too might work as "Story" sources as well. For after all, isn't every song a poem or story told to music?

How far is it to Bethlehem?

How far is it to Bethlehem?
Not very far.
Shall we find the stable room
Lit by a star?

Can we see the little Child?
Is He within?
If we lift the wooden latch
May we go in?

May we stroke the creatures there
Ox, ass, or sheep?
May we peep like them and see
Jesus asleep?

If we touch His tiny hand
Will He awake?
Will He know we've come so far
Just for His sake?

Great kings have precious gifts
And we have naught
Little smiles and little tears
Are all we brought.

For all weary children
Mary must weep
Here, on His bed of straw
Sleep, children, sleep.

God in His mother's arms
Babes in the byre
Sleep, as they sleep who find
Their heart's desire.

Carol of the Bells

Hark how the bells
Sweet silver bells
All seem to say
Throw cares away.

Christmas is here
Bringing good cheer
To young and old
Meek and the bold.

Ding dong ding dong
That is their song
With joyful ring
All caroling.

One seems to hear
Words of good cheer
From everywhere
Filling the air.

Oh, how they pound
Raising the sound
O'er hill and dale
Telling their tale.

Gaily they ring
While people sing
Songs of good cheer
Christmas is here.

Merry, merry, merry, merry Christmas
Merry, merry, merry, merry Christmas!

On on they send
On without end
Their joyful tone
To every home. Dong Ding dong ding... dong! Bong!

"Carol of the bells", also known as "Bell carol" and "Ukrainian carol" is based upon a Ukrainian carol composed by Mykola Dmytrovich Leontovych. Peter J. Wilhousky translated it to English.

The Little Drummer Boy

Come, they told me
Pa rum pum pum pum
A new born King to see
Pa rum pum pum pum
Our finest gifts we bring
Pa rum pum pum pum
To lay before the King
Pa rum pum pum pum
Rum pum pum pum
Rum pum pum pum
So to honor Him

Pa rum pum pum pum
When we come.

    Little Baby
Pa rum pum pum pum
I am a poor boy too
Pa rum pum pum pum
I have no gift to bring
Pa rum pum pum pum
That's fit to give our King
Pa rum pum pum pum
Rum pum pum pum
Rum pum pum pum
Shall I play for you
Pa rum pum pum pum
On my drum.

    Mary nodded
Pa rum pum pum pum
The ox and lamb kept time
Pa rum pum pum pum
I played my drum for Him
Pa rum pum pum pum
I played my best for Him
Pa rum pum pum pum
Rum pum pum pum
Rum pum pum pum
Then He smiled at me
Pa rum pum pum pum
Me and my drum.

    "The little drummer boy" is based on a Czech Christmas carol called, "The carol of the drum". Katherine K. Davis translated it to English.

We Three Kings Of Orient

We three kings of Orient are
Bearing gifts we traverse afar
Field and fountain, moor and mountain
Following yonder star.

O star of wonder, star of light
Star with royal beauty bright
Westward leading, still proceeding
Guide us to thy perfect light.

Born a King on Bethlehem's plain
Gold I bring, to crown Him again
King forever, ceasing never
Over us all to reign.

O star of wonder, star of light
Star with royal beauty bright
Westward leading, still proceeding
Guide us to thy perfect light.

Frankincense to offer have I
Incense owns a Deity nigh
Prayer and praising, voices raising
Worshiping God on high.

O star of wonder, star of light
Star with royal beauty bright
Westward leading, still proceeding
Guide us to thy perfect light.

Myrrh is mine, its bitter perfume
Breathes a life of gathering gloom
Sorrowing, sighing, bleeding, dying
Sealed in the stone cold tomb.

O star of wonder, star of light
Star with royal beauty bright
Westward leading, still proceeding
Guide us to thy perfect light.

Glorious now behold Him arise
King and God and Sacrifice
Alleluia, Alleluia
Sounds through the earth and skies.

O star of wonder, star of light
Star with royal beauty bright
Westward leading, still proceeding
Guide us to thy perfect light.

Up on the Housetop

Up on the housetop reindeer pause
Out jumps good old Santa Claus
Down through the chimney with lots of toys
All for the little ones
Christmas joys.

Ho, ho, ho!
Who wouldn't go!
Ho, ho, ho!
Who wouldn't go!
Up on the housetop
Click, click, click
Down through the chimney
With good Saint Nick.

First comes the stocking
Of little Nell

Oh, dear Santa
Fill it well

Give her a dolly
That laughs and cries
One that will open
And shut her eyes.

Ho, ho, ho!
Who wouldn't go!
Ho, ho, ho!
Who wouldn't go!
Up on the housetop
Click, click, click
Down through the chimney
With good Saint Nick.

Next comes the stocking
Of little Will
Oh, just see what
A glorious fill
Here is a hammer
And lots of tacks
Also a ball
And a whip that cracks.

Ho, ho, ho!
Who wouldn't go!
Ho, ho, ho!
Who wouldn't go!
Up on the housetop
Click, click, click
Down through the chimney
With good Saint Nick.

"Up on the housetop" was composed by Benjamin R. Hamby in 1860. This was the first secular American Christmas song.

The Twelve Days of Christmas

On the first day of Christmas
My true love sent to me:
A partridge in a pear tree.

On the second day of Christmas
My true love sent to me:
Two turtle doves
And a Partridge in a pear tree.

On the third day of Christmas
My true love sent to me:
Three French hens
Two turtle doves
And a Partridge in a pear tree.

On the fourth day of Christmas
My true love sent to me:
Four calling birds
Three French hens
Two turtle doves
And a Partridge in a pear tree.

On the fifth day of Christmas
My true love sent to me:
Five golden rings
Four calling birds
Three French hens
Two turtle doves
And a Partridge in a pear tree.

On the sixth day of Christmas
My true love sent to me:
Six geese a laying
Five golden rings
Four calling birds
Three French hens
Two turtle doves
And a Partridge in a pear tree.

On the seventh day of Christmas
My true love sent to me:
Seven swans a swimming
Six geese a laying
Five golden rings
Four calling birds
Three French hens
Two turtle doves
And a Partridge in a pear tree.

On the eighth day of Christmas
My true love sent to me:
Eight maids a milking
Seven swans a swimming
Six geese a laying
Five golden rings
Four calling birds
Three French hens
Two turtle doves
And a Partridge in a pear tree.

On the ninth day of Christmas
My true love sent to me:
Nine ladies dancing
Eight maids a milking
Seven swans a swimming
Six geese a laying

Five golden rings
Four calling birds
Three French hens
Two turtle doves
And a Partridge in a pear tree.

On the tenth day of Christmas
My true love sent to me:
Ten lords a leaping
Nine ladies dancing
Eight maids a milking
Seven swans a swimming
Six geese a laying
Five golden rings
Four calling birds
Three French hens
Two turtle doves
And a Partridge in a pear tree.

On the eleventh day of Christmas
My true love sent to me:
Eleven pipers piping
Ten lords a leaping
Nine ladies dancing
Eight maids a milking
Seven swans a swimming
Six geese a laying
Five golden rings
Four calling birds
Three French hens
Two turtle doves
And a Partridge in a pear tree.

On the twelfth day of Christmas
My true love sent to me:
Twelve drummers drumming

Eleven pipers piping
Ten lords a leaping
Nine ladies dancing
Eight maids a milking
Seven swans a swimming
Six geese a laying
Five golden rings
Four calling birds
Three French hens
Two turtle doves
And a Partridge in a pear tree.

"The twelve days of Christmas" are the days between the birthday of Jesus (December 25) and the day of the Epiphany, when the baby Jesus was visited by the wise men (January 6).

We Wish You a Merry Christmas

We wish you a merry Christmas
We wish you a merry Christmas
We wish you a merry Christmas
And a happy New Year.

Glad tidings we bring
To you and your kin
Glad tidings for Christmas
And a happy New Year!

We want some figgy pudding
We want some figgy pudding
We want some figgy pudding
Please bring it right here!

Glad tidings we bring
To you and your kin
Glad tidings for Christmas
And a happy New Year!

We won't go until we get some
We won't go until we get some
We won't go until we get some
So bring it out here!

Glad tidings we bring
To you and your kin
Glad tidings for Christmas
And a happy New Year!

We wish you a Merry Christmas
We wish you a Merry Christmas
We wish you a Merry Christmas
And a happy New Year.

Glad tidings we bring
To you and your kin
Glad tidings for Christmas
And a happy New Year!

"We wish you a merry Christmas" is a traditional Christmas song whose origin can be traced back to the 16th century.

Personal Note:

I was taught to perform many of these seasonal songs in Choir and Madrigals through Middle School and High School. While this training was "questionable" to me at the time I did enjoy singing and the training I was given has served me in many ways other than in song. That was my first taste of public performance and I learned to enjoy that as well.

I strongly suggest that if you have no training is music or have never spoken before an audience; you should join any local community classes, theatrical clubs, Storytelling groups and Speech/Toastmaster groups to learn to be comfortable in front of an audience. It will help you to become a more rounded performer.

Santa and the Use of Magic in a Visit

How to reinforce the idea that magical things happen around Santa

Santa is not a magician but magical creatures surround him in his daily life and magical things happen around him constantly. The use of selected magic effects in the Santa setting only helps to establish Santa is "real".

Little things can make a magical moment happen with very little effort or preparation on your part. I will describe several easy yet effective magic effects that will take very little practice but will deliver that moment of "Surreal" to your audience. That moment when the eyes go round and the audience both young and old stop and look hard at you and say "You are real!" simply because you bolstered their sense of fantasy and helped them suspend their disbelief for just a moment.

These effects range from the very simple to natural skills you can learn to gimmicked props used to illustrate a story being told.

Rope Magic

With items you can find in the craft store and around the home.

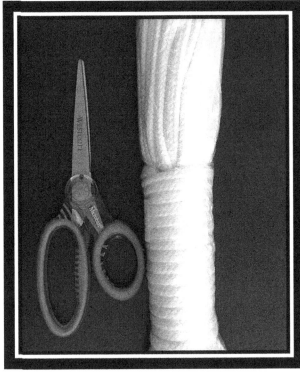

With easy to obtain items such as a sharp pair of scissors, some ¼ to 3/8-inch cotton rope and perhaps a brass macramé ring or two, you have hours of material to perform!

I am not going to describe how to perform the various effects I mention in this book but will give their names and that will give you the ability to look it up. I will be demonstrating the effects and how they are performed during the lecture in the class.

You will be able find and purchase these effects in any magic store or over the internet either as a "stand alone" effect or as part of an instructional such as a DVD on Rope Magic.

When using any rope you should first prepare the rope by "coring" it. This makes the rope suppler and easier to handle. If using nylon it is helpful to sear or melt the ends before using so they do not unravel.

As with any skill, the more you practice, the better the end result will be. Magic and Music are much alike! Both start with "M" and both end with "c". Anyone can make noise on a musical instrument but it takes practice to make music! Likewise anyone can do a "trick" but it takes practice to be magical.

The first would be the "Professor's Nightmare" in which 3 pieces of rope, all of different lengths become the same length and then go back to three different lengths. This is particularly nice in a "Santa" presentation when using red & white striped nylon rope.

The second would be "Cut and Restored Rope". You take a piece of rope and apparently cut it in half. You then "restore" the rope by tying the rope back together making it neat by trimming the ends down.

After some byplay with the audience you are "forced" to reveal the knot in the middle of the rope where upon the knot is shown to move up and down the rope at will. (It's a "slip" knot!) After the knot has been "vanished" and the fully restored rope has been displayed, for the very end blow off of this you can use a Christmas "mouth coil" (Green and Red color) as the "blow off" ending of the effect. There are at least 3 different endings to this particular effect, which allows you to keep the audience (children) guessing.

Knot tying routines

"Hunters mystery knot" this is a topographical impossibility effect that David Copperfield used in hospitals to help patients recovering from injury develop fine motor skills.

All you need is a piece of rope or cord about 36 inches in length. The brass ring is used in this effect to "prove" you never let go of either end at any time.

"The Shoelace Knot" seen in the Jerry Lewis movie "The Geisha Boy" uses the same length of rope or cord used in the "Hunters" effect. Very simple to do, but very deceptive.

"Two-handed Double Knot tying" is just that. Tie two knots with both hands without ever letting go of the rope. An easy "throw away" effect to help bridge from the previous knot tying effects to the next one.

"3-4 knots tied simultaneously" by looping the rope into your hand until you have it all coiled, simply retain the end and toss the coils out to form as many knots as there were coils!

"Single hand Knot" while holding the rope with one hand you simply reach down and pull out the knot! Can be done with either hand or both at the same time.

Each of these routines can be used standalone "throw away" or as part of a larger routine to illustrate how important knot tying is when handling Reindeer. Unless you want to illustrate how "Knotty" someone can be and still not make the list!

Gimmicked Rope effects

There are pure skill effects that take a moderate amount of practice and then there are what is called "Self-Working" or "Gimmicked" effects using special equipment. While I generally avoid such, there are a few worth mentioning.

Most involve the use of magnets, mechanical connecters or very specific handling and "patter" to accomplish their effect.

"Magnetic rope" a nice "one shot" effect where you have a long rope about 3 feet long and a short rope about 12 inches in length. The short rope will be tied around some small object like a card, plastic toy or nonferrous bell and placed in a bag. There is a strong magnet inside the end of each rope and you demonstrate your "skill" at "roping" a Reindeer by lowering the long rope into the bag while twirling and jiggling it around. What you are actually doing is bringing the 2 magnets into contact where they join together. You then gently pull the "tied" item out of the bag for all to see!

Rope Magnets can be purchased at any Magic store.

Squeakers – Or how to make any toy talk!

Squeakers have been a staple of Clowns and Magicians for many decades. They allow you to make a sound come from anything!

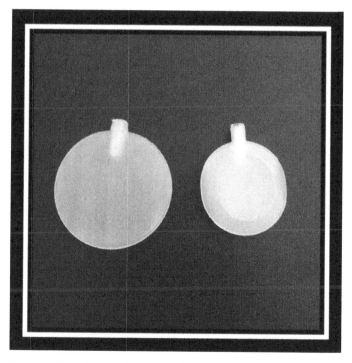

There are many ways you can use a Squeaker and again the only limit is your imagination! I will give you some of my favorite examples of use after these important words! You will get your greatest effect from Squeakers by using them in pairs. One in each glove located in the palm of the hand with the sound nozzle pointed outward away from your thumb.

This way you can show your gloved hands "empty to the inspection of the children! Do not let a child grab your hand and start squeezing it to find the device. You can allow them to inspect and push at your fingertips.

Uses for the Squeaker:

A child comes up and you ask him/her "Have you been watching Despicable Me?" when the child answers in the affirmative ask them "Who is your favorite Minion? Kevin or Dave?" When you get your answer, simply say, "That's why you sound like a Minion!" and pat them on the head gently with the squeaker under your glove in the palm of your hand(s). Alternately you can pat their shoulders like a Bongo Drum.

A child comes up clutching a teddy bear or the most beat up stuffed toy you ever saw or any doll and ask them "Does your toy talk?" When the child shakes their head, ask to "see" the toy for a moment and squeak a part of it. When the child "Hears" the toy "talking" they will snatch it back and try to do as you did. Without success. You can turn this into a game by "borrowing" the toy again and "squeaking" it in a different spot. The child will lose their reluctance to interact with you as you continue to squeak what they cannot.

Afterwards the parents will come up and tell you "they have had that thing for years and never knew it squeaked!"

Make the tummy of a crying child squeak. They will generally stop their crying, look down and then look up at you with a puzzled look on their face. That is a sellable picture. It also distracts the child from their crying jag and can lead to getting interacting and smiling with/at you.

Make different items within reach squeak. The back of the chair, one of the large props, different parts of the set like the line stanchions or direct your gaze at a particular part of the floor and using the tip of your boot, press down while you squeak your squeaker. The human ear cannot tell accurately where a sound is coming from, only direction. If you focus your attention on an object when squeaking it, the audience will "hear" that object "squeak"!

Explain that "Beanie Babies" have a way of being checked for counterfeit production. If it squeaks, it is a real one!

Tell someone wearing a silk coat that all "high end silk items have an emergency repair silk worm incorporated inside them" and then show them where it is.

Cause any object to "Squeak" at any time anywhere.

Ask if the fruit is fresh, squeak it and exclaim "Oh! I see it is!" This also works on any kind of foodstuff or beverage.

Ask if they knew about an insect known as a "No Seeum". Then show them where one was by squeaking/squishing it.

Wind your ears up by making a fist next to your ear and then make twisting motions with the fist as you *squeak*. Then offer to do the same for others.

Explain that the picture frame they are buying (or other item) has a very "Special" feature and then squeak it.

Finally ask if the children have washed up before coming to see you? Give them a Squeak and say "Yup! Squeaky-clean!"

Magnetic Rings

Magnetic rings are another item you can wear under your gloves that give you amazing opportunities to have unusual things happen in the course of normal conversation.

If you wear one of these rings on each hand (I prefer the second joint of the middle finger) again under your gloves, you can then have items such as "Sleigh Bells" appear out of "empty" hands.

The effect works like this, you pass your palm down gloved hand over a supply of bells. The magnetic ring will pick up a bell and thanks to the glove material, not make a noise or "talk". Keeping your fingers together and your hand flat, palm down, you then bring your hand to your body and rotate your wrist to bring your palm to up to face you and keeping the bell away from the view of the visitor. With your other hand shown empty, bring your hands together and "Steal" the bell away from the magnet into your just shown empty hand.

Now show the first hand empty by simply showing the palm to the audience. Then ask the child "Would you like a Sleigh Bell?" The child will of course say, "Yes!" and simply open the hand holding the bell you stole. From the viewpoint of the child, Santa just produced a bell from nothing!

Gold and Silver

Gold and Silver is a "one ahead" effect using 3 shells and a gold/silver "sun & moon" coin and a regular gold coin. The coins and shells nest together to appear to be only 2 coins.

I use this effect to illustrate the story of the Three Sisters that St. Nicholas saved from slavery by giving them a dowry. To perform this you will also need 4 small stockings and a rod  to hang the stockings from about 24 inches in length.

With an elf or child holding the rod with the stockings hung from it, you proceed to tell the story of the 3 sisters that lacked a dowry. You show the two coins in your hand and as you tell how St. Nicholas tossed money through the window into a stocking you remove one of the shells and place it into the first stocking. You then open your hand to show you still have 2 coins. You then continue the story and every time St. Nicholas tosses money into a stocking, you take a "coin" from your hand and put it into another of the stockings. After each time you do this, you then open your hand to show you have two coins still.

On the last time you fill the 4th stocking and finish the story, you then show your hands empty and tell them that this why Santa always has just the right number of gifts to leave.

Gold & Silver is sold through Magic Makers and found in magic shops everywhere.

Santa's little magic bag

This is a utility prop called a "change bag" and with it you can do a number of things. I use it to "force" the choice 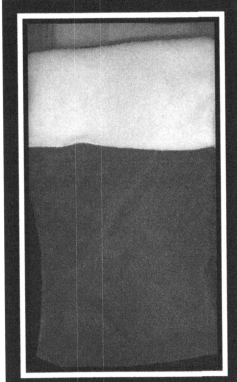 of ringing bells or non-ringing bells after a reading of the Polar Express. It can also "force" the selection of only peppermint candies after you have shown it contains multi colored and different flavored hard candies. The children always pull out peppermint. It can be used to produce a small gift after you turn the bag inside out showing it empty or you could use it to do a Christmas Blendo effect.

This type of effect also comes in a Christmas stocking shape and a Santa hat shape as well but they all operate the same.

Santa's Big Magic Bag

I had a "Santa Bag Emergency" and needed a new bag on short notice. I went to my trusted seamstress and told her my plight and she went back to the storeroom to look for fabric.

She came back with some 2 way stretch panne velvet and made me a quick bag but it was the size of a medium pillowcase! Used parachute cord for the drawstring. I explained it was way too small but she said, "Trust me."

Well I took that little bag and started putting the gifts into it on my first stop of the day. The more I put into the bag, the more it stretched! What started out as a 22-inch by 32-inch bag was soon 3 foot wide and over 4 foot tall when filled to capacity!

I made my entrance and everyone saw the "Big Bag" full of gifts and as I handed out the gifts the bag shrank back down to its original size. At the end of the visit, I picked up my now much smaller bag, folded it in half-length wise and then in half width wise and thrust it under my belt.

Every person in that room was amazed at how Santa's bag had shrunk down to a smallish pillow case size!

The agency I was working for called me the next day and told me about the feedback and said keep the magic bag in the show!

Paper Hat Tears

This is a throwaway effect that can be done at any point in a performance. Select a child or adult to be the recipient of the Hat and have them "Help You" make it.

You show 2 sheets of tissue paper. 1 red and 1 white. Ask them what color they are from the "helper" and when they say "Red and White" you raise the red sheet and say "White?" then the white sheet and say "Red?" When the helper says "No, the other way around!" you reverse the order but get the colors wrong again. You can do lots of little by play with this as you interact. You tear the two sheets in half giving the helper one half and you keep the other half. Again there is some by play for humorous effect. You collect all the pieces and crumple them up into a ball. Then from your fist you unfold a beautiful paper Santa Hat or Mrs. Claus Bonnet and place it on the head of the helper. You end up clean with nothing left in your hands.

There are many effects that fit in a Santa visit and that simply means you have to decide what type of effect you wish to have in your show. As I believe that less is more, I try to keep the effects to a minimum and of a small nature.

Several other effects do lend themselves to the Santa experience such as a Sponge balls routine. Look for "30 tricks and tips with sponge balls. This DVD comes with a set of 4 two inch red balls to start with. Sponge balls come in a variety of colors and size. Blue, Red, Green, Yellow, Orange, Purple and Black.

For Rope Magic look for 30 tricks and tips on Rope Magic also from Magic Makers.

If you wish to pull coins out of children's ears, you could get a copy of "Modern Coin Magic" 4 DVD set also from Magic Makers and learn the basic natural finger palm and the thumb clip palm and combine those two tools with the French Drop and the English Drop.

You will need "Band Gloves" that have traction dots on them so you can control the coins while wearing white gloves. If doing the coins bare handed, an easy "cheat that coin workers use is "Corn Huskers Lotion". Just a couple of drops rubbed into your hands will soften your skin and make it ever so slightly tacky as this hand lotion has glycerin in it and that will make it easier to handle the coins as you gain confidence.

You will find these items or similar ones on Amazon much less expensive than if you go to a magic store and purchase but receiving instruction by doing so.

It takes 15 minutes a day per effect for 10 days to "Own" the effect. That means to do the effect without looking or failure. So in theory, you could spend an hour each day for 10 days and master 4 effects in that time. You practice in front of a mirror so you can see how it looks from the audience point of view.

Since this is not "You" making the magic happen but it is happening around you, try to look as if you are just as amazed and amused as the rest of the audience as it happens.

Pay attention to your body language as you do this. Relaxed, elbows bent, slightly leaned forward with a curious look on your face as it happens. Look out to the viewing audience as much as you watch the show yourself.

Choose the effects carefully with an eye towards what fits your type of Santa performance. Home visit would lend itself to effects that illustrate a story more than a standalone "Surprise!" effect. In a mall setting you might look for a production kind of effect like a 8 inch Mirror box decorated like a present or a change bag effect in the form of a Santa hat, Stocking or small Santa bag. These could be pulled out at need and used to do a quick effect to amaze the children while the printer is loaded.

The corporate type event would possibly use a large "Tip Over Box" again decorated as a present on a roller trolley. This would be a "Grand Entrance" opening production of the CEO of the business. You roll the giant gift out and show it empty to the audience. Then you open the top and the CEO comes up out of the gift you rolled out and begins to present the Christmas bonuses to the audience.

There are several other effects in each of the different styles of Magic presentation that would fit everything from close intimate effects illustrating a story in a home visit to a "Play Big" throw away Parlor effect all the way up to a full blown Stage effect for a corporate event. By going into a Magic Store and discussing the setting and desired end, you can get a good idea of what might work for you out of the large number of effects available.

"Tip!"

"Odin the leader of the Norse Gods was a "Gift Giver" on December 25th. He rode his flying 8-legged White horse named Sleipnir or he drove his Chariot pulled by Reindeer.

Odin's son Thor also delivered gifts wearing a long white beard and wearing his Red Armor riding his Chariot pulled by 2 White Goats."

"Tip!"

"A smile does more than light up your face! If you let it reach your eyes it will engage the people you are visiting. It will also alter the way you sound as the smile shifts the nasal cavities making your voice sound "lighter" even over the phone it will make a big difference! Smiles are also contagious! If you give your smile to someone, they in turn will pass it on.

"Tip!"

"Always practice performing in front of a mirror. When practicing at first, put your suit on. This will help you "See" your Santa character as you do the exercises. When you put on the suit, you also put on the character and anything that does fit with your character should be eliminated."

"Tip!"

Rudolph the Red-Nosed reindeer began in the department store called Montgomery Ward in 1939. Copywriter Robert L. May wrote the story. Then singer/Cowboy actor Gene Autry immortalized Rudolph with a song in 1949. 1964 brought us the Rankin-Bass television show all about Rudolf as well.

"Tip!"

"There are many carols and songs and poems that can be used in your story telling program. One reason to have so many is to have the material ready if you need it to lengthen a visit (stall) to accommodate the Host in their desire to have everyone present to enjoy at least part of the visit. Another equally important reason is to have a new program of stories each year or at least 1 or 2 new stories when you are doing a repeat visit every year."

"TIP!"

Make sure the child is of an appropriate age to receive such a gift. Also make sure the bell is of large enough size it does not constitute a choking hazard to the child! With all three devices in play, Rocco's Delite, Squeaker and magnetic rings, you can perform quite a few little "magical" happenings during a visit that "Just happen around Santa for some reason".

"Tip!"

"Practice any magic effect in front of a mirror for 15 minutes a day. Do that for 14 days and you will "own" the effect. Your presentation should be able to do the motions required to perform the effect without looking at your hands and your movements should be smooth and natural.

Once you have mastered the first effect, move on to the next in the same way. In six weeks' time you will have mastered the 3 "hand" effects and be able to use them with ease. Remember to practice each effect at least once every week and before you do a performance. You could speed up your learning curve by studying all three effects for 15 minutes a day each. That would be 45 minutes to an hour daily you would have to devote for a 14-day period but in the end the results would be the same.

By adding a new effect carefully selected to fit our performance, you will have a varied and wonderful number of little "things that happen around me" moments that you will be able to do at a moment's notice."

"TIP!"

Children and many grownups are inquisitive! You can allow them to gently "pinch" your fingertips and gently push them during their explorations. While they are doing this you can insert a bit of byplay into the situation. Bend your finger to show it is a "real" finger.

If they accuse you of having something on your finger, you can put the finger in your mouth and then wipe it off on your pants and then continue to squeak objects. Finally you can caution them not to "Pull my finger" as that might well lead to a different kind of sound!

"TIP!"

By staring at the object you are "Squeaking" you direct the attention of your audience to that point, as they will look where you are directing your gaze.

Always work with your index finger extended and the rest of your fingers curled into your palm. A very slight movement of your curled fingers will cause the Squeaker in your palm under your glove to squeak!

To hide that motion, you move the tip of your finger onto the spot you wish to make the noise.

In the study of misdirection, a large motion (moving your finger to the spot to be squeaked) will disguise and cover a small motion (that of your curled fingers compressing the squeaker to operate it). DO NOT be anything but playful and curious when performing this "effect". Remember! You are not actually making the noise! You are not a magician!

Santa is very old! He is around all kinds of toys and wondrous devices/creatures/things. He has learned where all the "Squeaky Spots" are. That's all. Remember to be just as amazed as your audience when you "find" those spots!

"Tip!"

In 1750, Christmas Trees appeared in homes across Germany! Decorated with ornaments and candles to light it, the Christmas tree remained a localized tradition until German immigrants started decorating trees in Pennsylvania during the 1820s.

The tradition was then introduced to England in 1848 when Germany's Prince Albert married Queen Victoria and Christmas Trees were placed in the Palace.

"Tip!"

Rudolph the Red-Nosed Reindeer actually has cousins! Rangifer Tarandas are a breed of reindeer that actually have Red Noses!

"Tip!"

Under no circumstances ever "squeak" a child's nose or ear. If there is a sibling, they will reach over and twist the appendage 180 degrees to duplicate the effect. In the case of the nose you will then have a crying child with a bloody nose, a second child pointing at you and a very angry parent looking for the reason their child is injured!

Just like the light up thumb tips such as "Rocco's Delite" you will get your greatest effect from Squeakers by using them in pairs. One in each glove located in the palm of the hand with the sound nozzle pointed outward away from your thumb.

This way you can show your gloved hands "empty to the inspection of the children! Do not let a child grab your hand and start squeezing it to find the device. You can allow them to inspect and push at your fingertips.

"Tip!"

"The poem "A visit by St. Nicholas" Clement C. Moore is credited for authoring in 1822 where it was recited at a party given by Moore.

One of the guests, a young woman, copied the work for her own pleasure and the following year, 1823, sent it into the Sentinel Newspaper in Troy New York anonymously. Published in the Sentinel December 23, 1823 the poem was a great success! It captured the public's imagination.

The poem's opening line-"Twas the night before Christmas" soon replaced the original title. Moore accepted authorship in 1844 but some historians believe Henry Livingston, a Revolutionary War veteran residing in Up State

New York may have actually written the piece as early as 1807."

"Tip!"

"There are many carols and songs and poems that can be used in your story telling program. One reason to have so many is to have the material ready if you need it to lengthen a visit (stall) to accommodate the Host in their desire to have everyone present to enjoy at least part of the visit. Another equally important reason is to have a new program of stories each year or at least 1 or 2 new stories when you are doing a repeat visit every year." A final good reason is in certain venues you will have to have several 15 minute, 20 minute, 30 minute and 45 minute programs that have entirely different material for your presentation such as corporate events or school programs. By having this array of performance options you keep your presentation fresh and you are far more versatile in your performance!

"Tip!"

Before stepping out into the public view, inspect your appearance and check yourself visually. Is your suit aligned correctly? Are your gloves clean? Does your fur need a quick brushing? Do you have anything left over from lunch in your beard? Is the Buckle of the belt in the right position? Do you have your Santa Glasses on?

This visual check will help you keep your best appearance and help avoid having left something on the table or by the chair.

"Tip!"

"The first mention of Mrs. Claus is in a short story titled "A Christmas Legend" authored by James Rees."

Image Enhancement

Pictured here are several different forms of theatrical makeup used to whiten beards and hair along with an example of rouge used to pink noses and cheeks. Go online

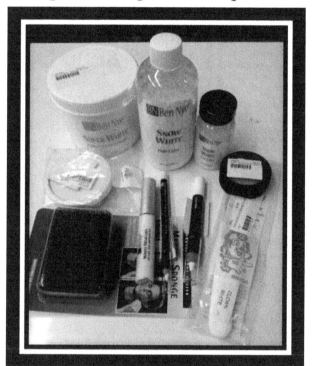

and Google to find "Ben Nye" makeup distributers in your area at most costume shops. Those shops that distribute Ben Nye will have someone there to help you with your particular needs and skin tone.

All of the materials pictured have been used at one time or another during my career as a Santa. Currently the White Mascara is what I keep in my kit to do "touch ups" on my mustache and eyebrows in between bleach sessions.

Other brands to look up would be Pro-Nose or Mehron or Kryolan. Theatrical make up is many times denser in color saturation than over the counter versions.

Even Mac. You will use less and the photos will look better using professional materials for the end result.

Theatrical Adhesives

Pictured here are the 4 basic theatrical adhesives used to attach "Traditional" beards to your face. From left to right they are:

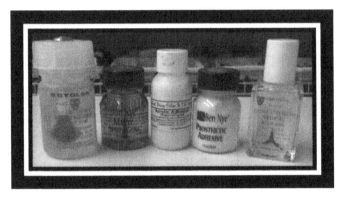

Water-soluble Spirit Gum

Matte (non water-soluble) Spirit Gum

Two forms of Prosthetic Adhesive (Acrylic copolymer contact cement) Medical Adhesive (Silicone based adhesive)

These materials are available under multiple brand names and various formulations of viscosity. The examples are also arranged from left to right in order of holding strength of the adhesive with Spirit Gum being the weakest and Medical Adhesive being the strongest.

You can Google them to find theatrical make up shops that carry these and their removers.

Do not use these adhesives without their removers and make sure the shop explains and demonstrates the proper application and removal before purchase.

Make Up and Santa Image Enhancement

From 87 to 95 part time and 95 through 2012 I worked in costume shops full time and helped new Santa's with their selections when they came in for suits and helped them with other aspects of their presentation. Theatrical make up was one of those areas I assisted them with. Both the Fun Corner in San Bernardino, California and Harlequin Costume in Ontario, California are full line Ben Nye make-up dealers. Most of the Santa's out there can use some help in enhancing their appearance. New (younger) Santa's have to cover dark hair and that can be done initially with bleaching which I recommend you go to a professional hair stylist for.

Spot coverage and touch up between bleaching is easily done with theatrical make up. You have several choices to work with. There is Super White Powder for setting Crème make-up or you can use Neutral Set if you don't want to go that white. You can apply Crème make up with different sized pencils or with a stipple sponge. Then you need to use the powder to "set" it, as Crème never dries. Next for touch ups is White Mascara which dries smudge proof (abrasion resistant) and water resistant (won't sweat off).

Easy application and very compact and portable. I use the Mascara to touch up my mustache and eyebrows and some Santa's use it to color their eyelashes as well.

For larger applications you can use Ben Nye's Snow White liquid hair color. This is made of water, alcohol, glycerin and dye grit too large to penetrate the hair follicle. You use a brush with bristles like a toothbrush to apply the well shaken liquid to clean dry hair and allow it to dry. The water and the alcohol evaporate and the glycerin holds the dye grit in place. You will need to use a topcoat spray of hair spray to keep the dye grit from rubbing off, as glycerin is not a very strong adhesive.

A different approach is to use hair styling gel (clear) mixed 50% with the Snow White liquid and applied to the hair and combed through. I have seen this done with a

Redken styling gel and the result was fantastic. Another choice is the Graphtobian white face paint stick. These are commonly included in the "Santa Kit" the photo company's supply to their set for the Santa. It is basically soap based face paint and will run if made wet (like with sweat).

Traditional bearded Santa's use adhesives to hold their beard in place. There again you have several choices. There is Spirit Gum (which comes in two types, water soluble and non-water soluble) with most using the Matte non water-soluble type. The next step up is Prosthetic Adhesive or Pros-aid, a water suspension acrylic co-polymer contact cement. Care must be taken when using Pros-aid. It must be allowed to dry completely clear before allowing the treated prosthetic to come into contact with the coated skin. Otherwise your sweat will cause the adhesive to re-subsume and the piece will fall off and you have to clean up and start over again. Finally there is Medical Adhesive which is a silicone based adhesive with very strong bonding properties.

Before using any adhesive you should clean your skin with soap and water and then use a good astringent like Witch Hazel to give you the best skin contact possible. When removing the piece, use the proper adhesive de-bonder called for and clean the piece gently to remove any excess adhesive and wash the piece with cleanser to remove any oils before setting it aside to dry before reuse.

Using Rouge

The use of a rouge to give you "Rosie cheeks" and a "Nose like a cherry" is also something to consider. You will need to select a rouge that works with your skin tone as unlike hair coloring, one rouge does not fit all. Use a small round powder brush to apply rouge to the "apple" of your cheeks in a "Nike" swoosh kind of application and just a light spin of the brush to the tip of your nose will do. You can then use a light spray of Ben Nye Final Seal Matte sealer spray to keep it from rubbing off on curious little fingers.

For those with "Oily" complexions, a light dusting of Neutral Set will knock down shine in photographs. Neutral Set looks white but it is actually colorless powder.

Finally you might try a very light application of Ben Nye Opal Ice glitter to your beard. Just a small amount run through your hair and then held in place with a light spray of hair spray will cause tiny highlights to show up in the photo graph. Almost like you had fiber optics woven into your hair. Opal ice is white but gives of a prismatic effect when in the light.

For older Santa's there are cover ups and neutralizers that will make age spots and discolorations fade away if needed. Again the idea is a little bit goes a long way. I recommend you visit a theatrical make up shop and get a consultation on what will help you best by matching what you need to your skin tone. I do not recommend you use street make up as it will not cover as well or last as long, not even Mac. The cost of Ben Nye is about half that of Mac but the density is about twice that of Mac. You "pays your money" and takes your chances.

You can find an authorized Ben Nye dealer near you by doing a Google search. Simply enter Ben Nye Makeup and your zip code to the search bar. Like this:

Ben Nye Makeup 92313

A listing of the nearest dealers will pop up and you can then arrange to visit the store when they have a makeup consultant there to show you how to use the product and select the proper colors for your skin tone.

Beard Care

 Pictured here is a bottle of Peppermint scented beard oil from *Sleigh Master Beard Products*. Along with the scent oil there are several more conditioning oils that help keep your beard strong and manageable. There are other scents as well but I prefer the Peppermint. All of the Sleigh Master products will keep your beard looking its best while keeping it smelling like Christmas! While the Beard oil gives the beard a light hold, the Beard Balm with 10 different ingredients giving a stronger hold to help control fly away hair. Beard Balm from SleighMaster.com comes in two styles; Normal and Firm.

Each bottle of Beard Oil and each tin of Beard Balm will last for 30 days of use.

To help your beard grow healthy, start using a Biotin supplement for Hair/Skin/Nail Health. Biotin is a B vitamin supplement you can purchase over the counter and it promotes hair and beard growth.

A final suggestion for Beard care and appearance would be to use Ben Nye Opal Ice glitter very sparingly on your beard after it has been treated with Beard Balm or Beard oil or both! Applied properly this will give you points of light in your beard that will show up in flash photography.

Alternately you could order "Santa's Star Dust" from Spangle the Clown that is a similar glitter as the Ben Nye but comes in an applicator bottle that makes the application easier. Always remember when it comes to Glitter, Less is More!

Invest in a small pair of scissors for mustache and "nose hair" trimming and a good magnifying mirror to keep in your kit for trimming and touch ups. In fact buy two pair of these scissors; one for home and one for your gig kit.

To curl your mustache you could use Bodacious Beard brand mustache wax or "Got 2 B" hair spiker. Bodacious Beard Mustache wax is strong enough to ride your motorcycle with and not have the 'stache drop. Got 2 B will hold it up in a very stiff wind as well all day long until you wash it out. Too, invest in a good mustache brush.

Also invest in a quality Hair curling wand, Hand held Hair drier, a set of quality brushes and use a good conditioner like Joico K-PAK Reconstruct conditioner on both your beard and your hair. Ask your hair stylist about clean rinsing shampoos and any recommendations they may have for brushes, hair care tools and scissors.

As Santa, your beard is the main defining aspect of your character followed by your Suit. Keeping both clean, fresh, smelling good and in good repair is very important to your presentation!

Alternate Props for a Santa presentation

Beyond the magic shops and the Santa themed "Bling" stores, you can look for other items that will fit into the "Santa" global presentation. Keep an eye out all year long for those as you go through your daily life.

There is a fairly new themed group activity known as "Steam Punk" that is basically an alternate timeline reality based recreation group activity much like a Civil War reenactment group or a Renaissance Faire group but Steam Punk is more in line with the writings of Jules Verne and H. G. Wells and uses Steam as the primary power source for all the inventions rather than Electricity as our society does today. By applying steam to the element "Unobtanium" they channel forces much like that of electricity in fantastic ways.

The style of this uses a lot of Brass in construction and they also use a considerable amount of electronics buried under that brass to make Steam Punk laptops, Steam punk Ray guns, Steam Punk watches and so on that would fit very well into a Santa presentation. Well maybe not ray guns, but much of that style is being used in greater number by Santas today.

Also look at Harbor Freight ads from time to time. They carry small brass items as well such as a pocket sized Sun Dial that you could mount on a watch band/strap. This Sun Dial folds up flat but would make for a humorous "time check" for Santa.

Another such item would be the Brass multi-color filtered Sexton they have that is almost pocket sized. Quite attractive with the different colored lens filters that pop up like a Swiss Army knife. You could use this item to lead into stories about your Sleigh rides and how you navigate by "Shooting the North Star" with it.

You will find some rather off the wall items in Hall Mark Card stores close to Christmas time such as the Polar Express Reindeer Harness Bell all in chrome. This Acorn style bell is exactly like the one pictured in the Polar Express illustrations and is handy to have when telling that story. You will also find such items as the Merryokie (spelling?) that is a voice-changing microphone (elf voice) that plays music and has several saying in an "Elf" voice. It will also act as a voice amplifier in a small way. The folks at Hall Mark come out with new items every year that you can add to your presentation. Just be sure to have batteries handy!

Be sure to go through all the "seasonal" displays in specialty shops and places like Target and Wal-Mart in their seasonal decoration departments as it comes close to season you will find lights, props and toys that will help you in many different types of presentation and in gaining a child's interest and trust during a Photo shoot on set. Just about any small device that lights up or makes noise will capture their attention and facilitate a smile. Remember, it is not so much about our "look" as it is about making easier for the child to accept Santa as real.

Just as in knowing the stories and histories of the various traditions, you do not need to bring those all out into your one-hour performance visit. You do not need to bring all of your "props" along. Having them will allow you to "change out" each year so the visit is fresh for repeat performances year after year.

With proper care and handling all of these props should last for years of use. Make sure to pack them away in a cool place and remove any batteries before putting them into storage. If you can afford it at the time when you see the item, purchase two. One for a backup.

For those Steam Punk items, keep a small bottle of brass paint, a small bottle of black enamel paint, a few nice brushes, a bottle of paint thinner and some polish handy as well to keep them in tiptop shape. The really nice thing about Steam Punk, is if the item happens to break, just add a little piping, a few elbow joints and a bit of paint and your item will not only be good as new but unique as well. It is also a good idea to keep a small bottle of thick super glue in your kit as well as a set of very small screwdrivers for opening the battery hatches.

Keep all of these "Maintenance" items in a separate little toolbox along with any other little bottles of model enamel paint, striping tape and assorted odds and ends. That keeps them all in one place and you never know when you might want to make a new prop for your presentation.

"I Have Been Good!"

This is to Certify that

_____

Having successfully completed the year
studying hard and doing the chores,
while minding what the parents say,
brushing the teeth and playing well and sharing with others,
eating all the vegetables including but not limited to broccoli,
lima beans and Brussel Sprouts, turning the TV off when
nobody is watching it

is hereby awarded this

Certificate of Excellence

and, shall be awarded the title of

"Good!"

Completed on _____

_____

Santa Claus Esq.

How to use this information

You will be "roleplaying" the character of Santa Claus and so you will need some of this information to make your portrayal "Real" for the audience. Performing a character is much more than putting on a suit and boots. You must "put on" the character as well.

Imagine portraying President Lincoln without knowing the details of his life and deeds. At best you would be President Lincoln with Amnesia or extreme dementia.

Part of taking on a role is learning all there is to know about the history of the character and the times he or she lived in. The more you know about the minutia, the personal habits, the company kept, the successes and the failures, all the details and over all history of the character you are trying to portray. So having as much information as you can is a way to bring your portrayal to "life" in the eyes of your audience.

From your first appearance at the door to your final goodbye and your exit out the door, every moment has been meticulously planned and researched. Your story telling program is structured organically so you can cut or extend it. The same goes for your entire show! The hardest part after timing your program is the exit.

The background material, histories of traditions and articles of facts that apply to the Santa Character will help you develop your presentation giving it greater depth and make it far more believable. You will become "Real" in the eyes of your audience both young and old.

Sketch out the frame work of your presentation and use the Companions, the Elves, the Reindeer, Mrs. Claus to highlight the points of that frame work and then further flesh it out using the various traditions involving the history, the traditions of the Christmas tree, the Candy Cane, The lights on the tree, and of course NORAD to make your presentation come alive!

Add these various facts and traditions to your presentation with an eye toward making the "Whole" work for you. In the same way, start with the basic Suit and Boots and then one at a time add to the image those items of "Bling" that actually work with your presentation. A hatpin, a Key on the belt, Bells on your bag or on a strap that you either wear or carry. By adding these physical accessories one at a time you build your image and make it unique to you. You invest in a custom leather Belt, put bells on your boots, add a pouch to your belt, add a little magic to your routine, collect books to add to your "story time" program, the possibilities are almost endless and if you just go out and buy everything your knees would buckle and all anyone will see is a shuffling mound of Props, Books and bling hung like ornaments on a tree without a plan.

Carefully consider each item you add to your presentation before you buy it. Once a year look over the entire presentation with an eye to changing it or tweaking it to fit your style of performance. Change out the books you carry from year to year to keep the program fresh. In the same way change out or add to your story telling program. Apply this to all of your presentation starting with the bling and ending with the suit.

Always remember you are not just putting on a suit to be Santa, you are slipping on an entire Character portrayal. You need to be comfortable in that character to present it realistically as a living reality. This will mean your character will evolve over time. Have Fun!

Thomas Nast

Thomas Nast was an illustrator and caricature of some fame and he created several iconic images such as the donkey and elephant images that depicted the Democrat and Republican political parties.

A German immigrant, Mr. Nast was on the staff of Harper's Weekly magazine from 1860 until the late 1880s. In 1863, Mr. Nast began to define the image of Santa through his illustrations. When Mr. Nast was asked to illustrate Clement C. Moore's poem "The Night before Christmas" for a book of children's poems, he gave the World a Santa who was far less stern looking than the ecclesiastical St. Nicholas of Europe.

While Santa was drawn as an elfin figure in red, he had a human quality to him as well. This Santa was kind, jolly and gentle.

To be sure there was a lot of subtle imagery that highlighted class differences (poking fun at Robber Baron industrialists) the image was recognized as a great tool for morale by President Lincoln. Abraham Lincoln asked Thomas Nast to draw a picture of this Santa visiting the Federal troops around a battlefield campfire on Christmas Eve. It was reported that Nast's drawing had a positive effect on the morale in the North that long, cold bloody winter.

For 22 years Thomas Nast kept adding to the details of his drawings of Santa in Harper's Weekly's December issues. Nast enhanced the legend of Santa with each presentation. Thomas Nast depicted Santa's workshop, created the "Naughty or Nice List", and in 1885 sketched Santa's home.

Also in that year's illustration you have two children looking at a map of the world and they are tracing the path of Santa's journey from the North Pole to the United States.

The following year, 1886, the American writer George P. Webster built upon this idea explaining that Santa's home and toy factory were hidden in the ice and snow of the North Pole.

We owe one more little thing to Thomas Nast. In the American language we have the word "Nasty" to describe something disagreeable in life. That was coined from Thomas Nast's name due to the many biting and sharp political and societal commentary cartoons he drew.

So while our modern day Santa owe much to the Coca Cola "Sunny" Sundblom ad artist and his depiction of the Coca Cola Santa image, it was Thomas Nast that lead the way to the modern American Santa Claus by giving us the "look", the location to call home, the Naughty or Nice list and the idea that Santa is Watching along with many of the other story foundations that define Santa today.

Haddon Hubbard "Sunny" Sundblom
June 22, 1899 to March 10, 1976

Sunny Sundblom was the artist hired to produce the Coca Cola ads, beginning in 1931 and continuing through the next 33 years to 1964!

A lesser-known Coke mascot in the 40s and 50s was Sprite Boy also invented and painted by Sundblom.

Sunny's final assignment was a cover painting for the 1972 Playboy magazine cover. While Sunny Sundblom was best known for his Santa pictures for the Coke Advertising campaign, he was also a very influential artist in several other fields as well.

His first offering in 1931 was titled "My hat's off to the Pause that refreshes". In 1932 an ad was run in the Ladies Home Journal titled "It will refresh you, too" and in the picture Santa is reading a note held in place on the mantelpiece with a bottle of coke and a bottle opener.

1933 saw "Away with a Tired Thirsty Face". 1934 has a recycled image from the first 1931 image but with the hat on and holding a whip titled "The pause that keeps you going- with a tingling buoyancy"

1935 repeats the title "It will refresh you, too" but pictures Santa with his coat off sitting on top of a ladder decorating a tree.

1936 repeats the image from 1931 but with the title "Me too" says old Santa. 1936 has the title Old Santa says: "Me too" with a picture of Santa without coat but wearing the belt sitting with a train and toys.

1937 titled "Give and take" say I showing Santa raiding an icebox for a coke and a chicken drumstick. 1938 titled "Thanks for the pause that refreshes" shows a small girl hugging a sitting Santa drinking a bottle of coke with his hat off.

1939 titled "And the same to you" shows the first Coke Santa wearing a Black belt. 1940 titled "Somebody knew I was coming" again shows a hatless Santa.

1941 titled "Thirst asks nothing more" shows Santa seated by a large Cooler filled with Coke. And his boots are once more brown as is his belt. He also lost the fur trim on his boots. 1942 has Santa standing on the front steps with his brown boots covered in snow titled "That Extra Something!" 1943 is a bit different in that it shows an American soldier being padded with a pillow and having a beard attached to his face by a Sargent with the title "Have a Coca-Cola=Merry Christmas…or how Americans spread the holiday spirit overseas"

1944 shows a picture of a living room scene with a couple of soldiers enjoying a family Christmas at home titled "Have a "Coke"=Merry Christmas….adding refreshment to holiday cheer". 1945 is also without Santa but a young family scene with a soldier laying on a sofa playing with a child and a wife watching from on her knees titled "Christmas together…Have a Coca-Cola….welcoming a fighting man home from the war"

1944 with Santa standing in snow next to a globe of the earth titled "Wherever I go". 1946 is another home family scene without Santa titled "Merry Christmas…Have a Coke…busy hands call for the pause that refreshes" 1947 has

Santa raiding a refrigerator sitting on a stool enjoying a bottle of Coke titled "Hospitality in your refrigerator"

1948 shows Santa in black boots and belt raiding the fridge again but introduces Spirit Boy as well titled "Where there's Coca-Cola there's Hospitality" and so it goes switching back and forth from black leather to brown leather but the message of hospitality and Santa at Christmas time continued through the entire run of the ads. As time passed the ads and Santa kept up with the times as well.

Character Development and Role Playing

All the world's a stage, And all the men and women merely players…

To portray the role of any character you must first learn about that character. In Clowning you do a "personality and character" sheet that describes your Clown's basic drives and character. In Magic a magician takes on the role that best suit his performance style and develops that style until it no longer fits his or her performance.

As Santa you have a rich history of stories and traditions to explore. Over 1700 years' worth!

But let's start with some basics. Role Playing is a valuable teaching tool, a means to develop characters in a book you might be writing or a style of games that were popular in the 70s, 80s, and 90s. Sales Managers use role-playing to help new sales people develop ways to counter sales resistance while talking to customers.

As a game form, you "generate" a set of "stats" that define the limits and abilities of your character but then you have to build a background for the character by giving it a name, a history, a set of likes and dislikes in short you develop the character and the more detail you give it, the more you identify with the character you are going to play. Let's go back the Santa example now.

You already have the name and description with the "Cheeks like roses, Nose like a Cherry, Eyes that twinkle, Dimples how Merry, Beard on his chin as white as the Snow" along with the overall description of being "Dressed all in fur from his head to his foot, a bundle of toy he had slung on his back" so that part is pretty well established even if we didn't have the Nast pictures from the 1860s and the Sundblom Coca Cola advertising pictures starting in 1931 through 1964 with his iconic "Coke Santa" image that is set in the public mind today. Sundblom also made several variations of that character including the "Work Shop" look with the coat off and the sleeves rolled up.

The following chapters will give you a wealth of background details and side notes that Santa would be expected to know. You do not have to go any deeper than the Ranking Bass Claymation stop action movies that play every Christmas season and indeed many start and stop right there in developing a Santa character that has depth and width. A Santa that actually "lives" in the living room he is visiting with the children that live there will use any and all information he can find to "Be" that Santa. You can use parts that appeal to you to make your character become Santa. In between the facts and dry information there will be little side notes that may help you make your "story" more "first person".

What influences created the "Western" Santa?

St. Nicholas is widely accepted and recognized as the inspiration for the modern "Western" Santa and in fact many people (including new Santas) believe that "Santa" and St. Nicholas are one and the same. While St. Nicholas is a large part of the "Santa Claus" character, there is much more to the "Santa" character than a Bishop that lived in Myra over 1700 years ago.

St. Nicholas was born in 270 AD and became the Bishop of Myra in 300 AD. (Also known as the "Boy Bishop") Under the Edict of Milan, Emperor Diocletian prosecuted and imprisoned St. Nicholas (then Bishop) in the year 303 AD.

He was later released by Emperor Constantine February of 313 AD. Nicholas attended the Council of Nicaea in 325 AD and died December 6, 343 AD, which is now celebrated as St. Nicholas day. Many countries in Europe and around the World have St. Nicholas traditions and stories that surround the Christmas holidays. These traditions and stories came to America when people immigrated to this country where they blended/mixed to eventually form the "Santa Claus" character.

Even the St. Nicholas Center recognizes "Santa" as a separate character.

"In the 1930s a group of lads dressed in Santa costumes introducing a new image and character, now referred to as the Coca Cola Santa."

That is just a little of the history of St Nicholas, but what about the "Other" Saint? I refer to St. Basil of Caesarea and his influence over the Orthodox Catholic religion and the Santa visits that occur starting December 31 and running through to January 14th. St. Basil the Great was born around 329-330 AD in Caesarea, Cappadocia and venerated in Eastern Orthodox Church, Oriental Orthodoxy and the Roman Catholic Church.

He received his formal education during 350-351 AD and was made Bishop June 14, 370 AD then passed away January 1, 379 AD.

January 1 is considered both the Feast day for St Basil and the "Christmas Eve" for most Orthodox branches of Christianity complete with visits from "Santa". For many reasons St. Basil has been acknowledged as the influence for the "Eastern" Santa. But there are other influences into the "Santa" character beyond these two Saints. Yes, be of open mind as there is much more to Christmas than you would think or were lead to believe.

For although the date of December 25th is a major High Holy Day for Christians of all type, some of our traditions came from much earlier than the birth of Christ. In fact many have no basis in the Christian religion at all. But they do give some of the story behind "Santa" and where he came from. This will be explored a little on following pages.

Christmas Themed Movies

The traditions of Christmas and the image of Santa have rapidly changed since the advent of motion pictures. In fact the image and tradition stories of Santa Claus have changed more in the last 80 years than the image and traditions of St. Nicholas has in the last 800 years. So for those days and evenings before the season truly begins and you need a little help getting into the spirit of the Season, here you go!

The Lemon Drop Kid – 1934 original

Holiday Inn – 1942

Christmas in Connecticut – 1945

It's a Wonderful Life – 1946

The Bishop's Wife – 1947

Christmas Eve – 1947

Miracle on 34th Street – 1947

A Christmas Wish - 1950

The Lemon Drop Kid –1951 remake

White Christmas – 1954 remake of Holiday Inn

Santa Claus – 1959

Santa Claus Conquers the Martians – 1964

Santa Claus is Comin' to Town - 1970

An American Christmas Carol - 1979

A Christmas Story – 1983

Mickey's Christmas Carol – 1983

It came upon a Midnight Clear – 1984

A Christmas Carol - 1984

Santa Claus The Movie – 1985

Scrooged - 1988

National Lampoon's Christmas Vacation – 1989

Home Alone – 1990

Yes Virginia, There is a Santa Claus – 1991 with Charles Bronson

Christmas in Connecticut – 1992 TV remake

Home Alone 2-Lost in New York – 1992

The Muppet Christmas Carol – 1992

Miracle on 34th Street – 1994 remake

The Santa Clause – 1994 Tim Allen

Jingle All The Way – 1996

The Preacher's Wife – 1996 remake of The Bishop's Wife

How The Grinch Stole Christmas – 2000 Jim Carrey

The Santa Clause 2 – 2002 Tim Allen

Elf – 2003

Bad Santa – 2003

National Lampoon's Christmas Vacation 2 - 2003

Surviving Christmas – 2004

Christmas with the Kranks – 2004

The Polar Express - 2004

Santa's Slay - 2005

The Santa Clause 3 The Escape Clause – 2007

Fred Claus -2007

Shrek the Halls – 2007

A Christmas Story 2 – 2012

Jingle All The Way 2 – 2014

Krampus - 2015

Each of these movies since 1934 has shaped and altered the public's awareness and vision of Christmas and Santa. At every new Santa release the image and story of Santa changed slightly and sometimes more so.

The "Christmas" movies that do not focus on Santa still have altered the basic image and form of the holiday. Since I grew up with this, I accept it but I must point out the process has been continuous and goes forward even today.

One recent example is the adaptation of the "Shrek the Halls" into a Mall photo set last year. Several of these $million + sets were built and placed across the country using a Shrek video presentation as part of the visit and some very high tech touch screen interaction.

Hallmark movies come out every year with new offerings that are heartwarming and funny. They also make commentary on the current issues of the day.

Alternate Names from Around the World

In no particular order I present some of the names of the gift givers from around the world. Most are local versions of St. Nicholas but not all.

Vietnam – Ong gia Noel (Christmas Old Man)

Venezuela – San Nicolas

Uzbekistan – Qor Bobo (Grandfather Snow)

U.S.A. – Santa Claus Hawaii – Kanakaloka

UK – Father Christmas and Santa Claus

Wales – Sion Corn (Chimney John)

Ukraine – Svyatyy Mikolay and Did Moroz

Turkey – Noel Babal

Syria – Baba Noel

Switzerland – Samichlaus

Sweden – Jultomtem (Santa Claus) Nissar/Tomte (Elves)

Sri Lanka – Naththal Seeya

Spain – Papa Noel

South Korea – Santa Kullosu (Santa Grandfather)

South Africa – Sinterklaas or Kersvader

Slovenia – Sveti Mraz or Sveti Nikolaj also Dedek Mraz

Serbia – Deda Mraz (Grandfather Frost) or Bozic Bata (Christmas Brother)

Russia – Ded Morez (Grandfather Frost)

Romania – Mos Cracium (Old Man Christmas) Mos Nicole (Old Man Nicholas) Mos Gerila (Old Man Frost)

Portugal – Pai Natal (Father Christmas)

Poland – Swiety Mikolaj (St. Nicholas)

Philippines – Santa Klaus

Peru – Papa Noel

Pakistan – Christmas Baba

Norway– Julenissen (Santa Claus) Julnisse(Danish Christmas elf)

Mexico – Santo Clos

Malta – San Niklaw (St. Nicholas)

Macedonia - Dedo Mraz

Lebanon – Baba Noel

Lithuania – Senis Saltis (Old Man Frost) Kaledy Senelis (Christmas Grandfather)

Latvia – Ziemassvetku Vecitis (Christmas old Man)

Japan – Santa-san (Mr. Santa)

Italy – Bobo Natale (Santa Claus)

Ireland – San Nicolas (St. Nicholas) Daidi na Nollag (Father Christmas)

Iraq – Baba Noel or Vader Kersfees

Indonesia – Sinterklas

Iceland – Jolasveinn (Yule Man) Jolasveinarnir (The Yule Lads)

Hungary – Mikalus (Nicholas) Telapo (Old Man Winter)

Holland/Netherlands – Sinterklaas (St. Nicholas) Kerstman (Christmas Man)

Haiti – Tonton Nwel

Greece – Aghios Vassilis (St. Basil)

Germany – Weihnachtsman (Christmas Man)

Georgia – Tovlis Babua or Tovlis Papa (Snow Grandfather)

France – Pere Noel

Finland – Santa Claus or Joulupukki

Ethiopia – Yagena Abat (Christmas Father)

Estonia – Jouluvana (Yule Elder)

Egypt - Baba Noel

Ecuador – Papa Noel

Denmark – Julemandcn (Christmas Man)

Czech Republic – Svaty Mikulas (St. Nicholas)

Croatia – Djed Bozicnjak (Grandfather Christmas)

Costa Rica – Colacho (St. Nicholas)

China – Shengdan la ren (Old Man Christmas)

Chile – Viejito Pasuero (Christmas Old Man)

Bulgaria – Arao Koneaa (Grandfather Christmas)

Brazil – Papai Noel or Bom Velhinho (Good Old Man)

Bosnia & Herzegovina – Djeda Mraz (Grandfather Frost)

Belgium – Sinterklaas or St. Niklass

Azerbaijan – Saxta Baba (Grandfather Frost)

Armenia – Gaghant Baba (Father Christmas)

Albania – Babadimiri

Afghanistan – Baba Chaghaloo

Greenland – Father Christmas

Moroco – Black Peter

While not a complete list, this does give you 65 countries and a combined 82 names for the Gift giver at Christmas time. These names and countries will give you a starting place to make your own stories or relate to visitors from one of those 63 countries.

In Celtic traditions it is custom to leave a candle in the window to welcome Mary and Joseph into your home for shelter. It is also custom to leave a bottle of Guinness and a mince pie for Santa. The Celtic traditional "Nature Folk" are modernized into elves.

Decorating with Holly & Ivy, Mistletoe and evergreen boughs dates back to the early Roman Empire.

Various "Homes" where Santa/St Nicholas lived were Spain-Norway-Finland-Iceland-Lapland and of course the North Pole has been Santa Claus's home since the 1860s.

First mention of Mrs. Claus

Mrs. Claus aka Mother Christmas in the UK was first mentioned in "A Christmas Story" in 1849 written by James Ree.

Mentioned again in the Yale Literary Magazine in 1851. Again in an account of a Christmas musicale at the State Lunatic Asylum in Utica, New York that included an Appearance of Mrs. Claus with a baby in her arms, danced to a holiday song.

More passing references in Harper's Weekly magazine in 1862 and in the comic novel "Metropolites" (1864) by Robert St. Clar. Mrs. Claus is a relatively new personality in the world of Santa.

In the Rankin-Bass 1970 movie "Santa Claus is coming to Town" Mrs. Claus began as the schoolteacher Miss Jessica in Somber Town.

Santa's Reindeer and Their Names

We all know about Santa's "A" team of 9 reindeer with Dasher, Dancer, Prancer, Vixen, Comet, Cupid, Donner and Blitzen along with Rudolph. But what about the "Other" teams?

In L. Frank Baum's "The Life and Adventures of Santa Claus" (1902) is included a list of 10 Reindeer, none of which match the names mentioned in "The Night Before Christmas".

Flossie and Glossie are Santa's favorites in Baum's book. Santa collects eight more reindeer in rhyming pairs:

Racer and Pacer

Fearless and Peerless

Ready and Steady

Feckless and Speckless

In Rudolph (1954) Fireball (Son of Blitzen) is introduced and we get to meet Clarice who becomes Rudolph's girlfriend.

In the 2002 South Park Christmas Special "Red Sleigh Down" when Santa's sleigh is shot down over Iraq, the "back up" team is sent to the rescue with Steven, Fluffy, Horace, Chantel, Skippy, Rainbow, Patches and Montel.

You can have fun naming reindeer but always remember the 9 members of the "A" team.

Means of Transportation

You know about the sleigh and the 9 reindeer but what of the "other" means of transportation?

Father Christmas rode a "Yule" goat.

Sinterklaas rode a white horse.

Odin rode an eight-legged flying horse named Sleipnir. Odin also drove a reindeer pulled chariot.

Thor rode his chariot wearing his red armor and long white beard pulled by two goats.

The Tomte ride a sleigh pulled by a Goat.

Pere Noel rides a donkey named Gui.

Father Winter rode a sledge pulled by two Boars named Donder and Blitzen.

The original eight reindeer names in Moore's poem were Dasher, Dancer, Prancer, Vixen, Comet, Cupid, Dunder and Blixem. The last two were in Dutch and were later changed to Donner and Blitzen (thunder and lightning in German).

Santa's Elves

First introduced in 1856 by Louisa May Alcott in her book "Christmas Elves". Elves are pictured in a workshop theme in Godey's Lady's Book with a front cover picture for the 1873 Christmas Issue showing Santa surrounded by toys and Elves.

Godey's was very influential to the birth of Christmas Traditions having widely shown the first circulated picture of a modern Christmas tree on the front cover of the 1850 Christmas issue.

In Altoona, Pennsylvania and communities in the Boston area, children celebrate Buzzlewitz Day on November 11.

According to the Lowther tradition, Buzzlewitz is the elf sent by Santa to collect children's Christmas lists. On November 11 each year at 11 pm, children leave their Christmas lists and a Snickerdoodle cookie on the Mantle or in the kitchen.

Buzzlewitz comes in the night and collects the lists. In return he leaves a mint and an acorn.

There are many Elves named in the 3 "Santa Clause" movies along with the other "Santa" centric movies that have come out lately over the last 20 years. Use those names or make up some of your own.

Now because of various recent movies including the 3 "Santa Clause" movies, "Elf" and "Fred Claus" to name just 5, we have seen examples of Toy Making Elves, Reindeer Handling Elves, Mission Control Elves, Santa Security Elves (like the secret service only shorter), Hot Chocolate making Elves, Baking Elves, DJ Elves, World Wide Naughty and Nice List monitoring Elves, Christmas list reading Elves, Ride along in the Sleigh Navigator Elves, Present Wrapping Elves, Coal Allocation Elves, Medical Elves, Fire Fighting Elves, Search and Rescue Elves, Covert Action Elves (infiltrating the Christmas population of Humans masquerading as children keeping their pointy ears out of sight in various ways), Accounting Elves, Research and Development Elves, Tree Decoration and Tinsel Elves…the list goes on and on.

In fact there appears to be a very complete Government (Benevolent Dictatorship under Santa), infrastructure and hierarchy in the Elf sub-culture from the Number 1 Elf (currently last known as Bernard) down through the Number 2 Elf in charge of the "Rules" all the way down to the smallest Elf that carries cookies around and offers them to Santa and others at need. Any Job category you might think of, you simply assign one elf as the Number One Elf for that job and then you have as many other Elves under #1 that do the work.

In the movie "Santa Claus is coming to Town" (1970) the first elf you meet was Dingle Kringle with his 4 brothers and Tanta Kringle.

With this structure example already in place, all you need do is make up your own names and MOS (specialty/occupation) for these Elves of yours and start plugging them into your Character background story(s).

As exampled in the previously mentioned movies, Elves also have a complex social interaction in their homes and social lives. They do not have to work 24/7/365 and there is even mention of Union Shop Stewards that make sure the working

Elves are not over worked, given Cookie and Hot Chocolate breaks along with other benefits. Housing, meals and transportation along with a quality medical plan and a generous retirement plan once they reach the option age of 1200 years of age is all provided under the most recent Union Contract dated 1860 and up for renewal in 3048.

Elves have been seen in Elf Taverns and they also like to watch and participate in Organized Sports although their ideas on Sports are slightly different from that of Humans. Their diet seems to be based upon food groups that would be very unhealthy for a human to consume for any long period of time. Candy Corn, Candy Canes, Cotton Candy, Sugar frosted Cereals, Maple Syrup, Corn Syrup, Soda (particularly fond of Coke Products and Mountain Dew but have been seen drinking Monster and Red Bull) Candied Yams, Sweet Potatoes, Hot Chocolate, Anything Chocolate, Gum Drops, Cookies, Brownies (the baked kind and not the related to Elves kind), Cakes, Pies, Sweet Bread products of all national origin such as Donuts and Danish, Fudge of any flavor but as noted before they seem to prefer Chocolate over other flavors and will swallow Gum.

It has been exceedingly difficult to get the Elves to eat regular vegetables in any quantity with the exception of Sugar Beets, Sugar Snap Peas, or anything with the word "Sugar" included in the name. Mrs. Claus has experimented in baking them into treats such as Zucchini Breads, Pumpkin Breads, the infamous (but quite chewy) Peanut Butter, Oatmeal, Raisin, Chocolate Chip, Lima Bean, Brussels Sprout, and Walnut cookies. They do enjoy fruits of all manners in raw form or baked. They will consume Dairy products such as Cheeses and Milk but again the preference is loaded more to Ice Cream, Whipped Cream and Yogurt. While they will drink wine on special occasions they tend to stay away from Beer preferring instead Mead when consuming alcohol on those rare times.

Proper care and feeding seems to be the only requirements other than a Job to do to make Elves Happy. All of life seems to be a game for Elves and since they have an exceedingly long lifespan (175 years is considered to be Very Young to be seriously involved in any form of work) that would seem to be a survival adaptation. Otherwise they would most likely exhibit the mannerisms and personalities of Dwarven kind and that of the Trolls. That of Dour, Grumpy and downright Mean.

Santa's Old World Companions and Other Creatures

You're not alone out there!

Well as you recall, Santa has his nine-member Sleigh team of reindeer, Mrs. Claus and a veritable army of Elves that keep things going up at the North Pole. But in the Old Country back in the day St. Nicholas had some others that helped him in various ways. This chapter will look at some of those "other" companions and creatures and give you some background on them as well. Let us start with:

Black Peter - found in the Netherlands, Belgium and Flanders Recently the subject of Lawsuits from the UN, Black Peter has become something of a misunderstood tradition. You see, Black Peter is the fellow that St. Nicholas used to send up and down the chimneys to deliver gifts to good children and punishment in various degrees to the naughty children. Today Black Peter delivers candy, cookies and gifts but in the early days he would also carry a birch switch to beat bad children with.

Very naughty children were stuffed into sacks and carried off to Spain where they would work in St. Nicholas's factory for a year and then returned home.

Back when this tradition started, St. Nicholas was supposed to have a home/toy factory located in Spain and Black Peter was a Moor from Spain. Also known as Swarte Pietr.

Combining his natural dark complexion from his Moorish Heritage with the black soot from the chimney and his name is very well explained. However the UN had filed suit over the tradition of Black Peter as being prejudicial against Africans.

Knecht Rupptrecht – first seen in 1668 he shows up in Northern and Central Europe particularly in Germany, Austria and Holland. Also known as Belsnickle, Pelznickle, Furry Thomas, Ru-Klas, Rough Nicholas. He seems to be derived from both Odin and St. Nicholas. He is sometimes known as the "Dark" side of St. Nicholas. He appears as a man with a black beard dressed in brown and black with a chain locked around his waist. A bit grubby, he performs much like Black Peter and carries a large bag of gifts. His job is to examine children on their knowledge of prayers and punish those found deficient.

Klaubauf – Austria

Accompanies St. Nicholas on visits December 5. He is a demonic Page dressed in rags and his purpose is to frighten children into better behavior.

Krampus- Found in Germany, Austria and Seattle Washington and occasionally at comic conventions.

Christmas devil/demon from Austria that goes with St. Nicholas on December 6th visits. In many ways is a bigger and nastier version of Klaubauf and Knecht Rupprecht combined.

One story has it that Krampus battled with St. Nicholas and lost. Krampus was then placed into servitude to St. Nicholas and served him well. While all of the "companions" administered discipline in the form of beatings with whips, switches and birch rods and occasionally would stuff particularly naughty children into sack or bundle them into baskets, Krampus was known for eating children that were very naughty sometimes stuffing them in a sack for later consumption. All of this apparently with the approval of St. Nicholas as they were always together on their journey to deliver gifts or discipline. While perhaps one of the worst of the Companions, Krampus was not the only former minion of Satan nor was he the only one to eat children as a form of punishment. Has his own movie released in 2015.

La Pere Fouettard aka Pere Fouchette-France

Takes his name from the French word fouet meaning birch rod. "Father Birch Rod" comes with Pere Noel "Father Christmas". Naughty children are beaten with the rod. Really bad children are bundled up and carried away in a basket. Pere Fouettard is no slouch in discipline though. He cuts the tongues out of children that lie to him.

Star Man – Poland

In Poland St. Nicholas visits on December 6th bringing gifts but on Christmas Eve Star Man comes to visit attended by the Star Boys. The Star Boys are all dressed fantastically as Wise Men, Animals or figures from the Nativity. Star Man examines the children in their catechism and brings them presents.

The Devil and Angel – Ukraine

On December 6, St. Nicholas comes to homes to visit with two companions. The Devil and an Angel. The trio of visitors come into the home and then listens to the parents about how terrible the children were the last year. Then they turn to the children and hear rebuttal. Once both sides have been heard, the three visitors consult and render judgment.

Naughty children receive a raw potato or lump of coal. Children that have been good receive a gold or silver coin.

The children then have to go door to door and show all the neighbors what they had received from St. Nicholas. Peer pressure is a powerful thing! They have from the 6th to Christmas Eve to correct their naughty ways and then they may get presents.

Frau Perchta - Germany and Austria

She hands out both punishments and rewards during the 12 days of Christmas (December 25 through January 6). Sinful children she rips out their organs and replaces them with garbage.

Gryla – Iceland

Mother of the Yule Lads. A hungry Troll that takes, kills, cooks and eats bad children! Married 3 times and has had 72 children including the "Yule Boys" aka Jolasveinar. Also lives with Jolakotturinn the Christmas Cat as a house pet. Gryla is perhaps the worst of the Companions but her children were no angles either. An interesting thing to note is 13 of her 72 children seemed to have become less Troll like and more Elf like over exposure to centuries of Christianity. I refer to the "Yule Lads" and the fact they have curtailed their beating of the slow, lazy or stupid and will engage in 13 days of gift giving. One day for each Yule Lad and the gift given each day reflects the personality of that particular Lad.

Jolakotturinn – Iceland

The Christmas Cat. Not a very nice kitty, will eat lazy children that do not do their chores.

Jolasvienar – Iceland

The Yule Lads, and there are 13 of them! Back in the day, they would cause mischief and harm around the farm but since the encroachment of Christianity these baker's dozen of troll sons also bring gifts. One on each Yule Boy's day and so you receive 13 gifts over 13 days if you are good!

Hans Trapp – Alsace and Lorraine region of France

Hans Trapp was a rich, greedy evil man that worshiped Satan and was excommunicated from the Catholic Church. He was exiled to live in a forest where he would disguise himself to look like a scarecrow by stuffing straw into his sleeves and pants. In the forest he would prey on children and eat them. Described as wearing dirty brown clothing with a long dark beard and a heavy chain locked around his waist.

Tomte – Norway-Finland-Sweden aka Nisse

Farm gnomes that over time took on the "Gift Giver" role. Starting out small gnomish figures, they grew taller and became more human in appearance. Modern names include Jultomte, Julnisse and Joulupukki. Drives a sleigh but it does not fly.

Mari Llwyd – Welsh Christmas Creature

Half man, half animal Origin unknown.

The person playing Mari Llwyd wears a white sheet bedecked with ornaments, Christmas balls, Holly and Tinsel with a huge headpiece resembling a horse head that covers the entire upper torso. Generally this creature prances around the town making noises and if it "bites" you, you are then required to pay a fine.

Klapparbock – Danish

A Danish version of Julbock but not a gift giver! More of a children frightener. A rather disagreeable Goat if there ever was one!

Julbock – Sweden

The Christmas Goat that delivered gifts in Sweden later to be replaced by Jultomten (gnome) Christmas elf that delivers gifts.

Schmutzli – Switzerland

Carries a bag of gifts for Samichlaus who brings Mandarin Oranges, cookies & nuts along with small gifts that are delivered into stockings hung on the 5th and 6th of December.

Hoteiosho – Japan

A Japanese Monk with eyes in the back of his head that gives gifts and travels with a Red-Nosed Reindeer.

Christkindl – Germany

Literally means "Christ Child" but is sometimes recognized as a very young appearing angel. Brings gifts and protects St. Nicholas. It is also the "root" for the name Kris Kringle.

Angels – Belgium, Germany, Poland, Austria

Various and many, Angels are companions of St. Nicholas protecting him from harm and occasionally sent to intercede on behalf of a child.

Sneguro Cka – Russia

Young granddaughter of Ded Moroz. Known as the "Snow Maiden" she arrives with her Grandfather delivered by a Troika of white horses.

Ded Moroz – Russia

Started out as an evil sorcerer that kidnapped children and held them demanding presents for ransom. St. Nicholas caused a change of heart and is now a reformed benevolent gift giver in much of the Slavic countries. Ded Moroz is the recognized gift giver covering the Russian Federation. While he is not "Santa" or St. Nicholas, Ded Moroz performs the function of Gift Giver across the Federation.

This is a partial list of "companions" and "creatures" that accompany St. Nicholas on his gift giving journeys. There are more but this will give you a start when you start developing your own stories from the past.

NORAD Tracks Santa and his Sleigh

In December of 1955 a Sears Dept. store ad ran in the Colorado Springs Newspaper with a typo in the phone number. The number was supposed to let children talk directly to Santa but instead of reaching Santa it went directly to the CONAD Commander- in Chief's operations "hotline".

The Director of Operations at that time, Colonel Harry Shoup told the Staff on Duty to check the radar for indications of Santa making his way south the North Pole and give the current location of Santa to the children that called.

NORAD replaced CONAD in 1958 but the tradition begun in 1955 continued to this day.

More than 12,000 emails and 70,000 phone calls from more than 200 countries around the world are answered by volunteers during the 36 hours that NORAD tracks Santa in his flight delivering presents to children around the world!

Media from all over the World rely on NORAD as a trusted source to provide updates on Santa's journey. Millions of people who want to know of Santa's whereabouts now visit the NORAD Tracks Santa website.

NORAD has a file on Santa and his Sleigh that contains Technical Data as follows:

Designer& Builder: K. Kringle & Elves Inc.

Probable First Flight: Dec. 24, 343 A.D.

Home Base: North Pole

Length: 75 cc (candy canes) / 150 lp (lollipops)

Width: 40 cc /80 lp

Height: 55 cc / 110 lp

Note: Height, Width and Length are without Reindeer.

Weight at Take Off: 75,000 gd (gumdrops)

Passenger Weight at Take Off: 260 pounds

Weight of Gifts at Take Off: 60,000 Tons

Weight at Landing: 80,000 gd (ice and snow accumulation)

Passenger Weight at Landing: 1,260 pounds

Propulsion: Nine (9) rp (reindeer power)

Armament: Antlers (purely defensive)

Fuel: Hay, oats, and carrots (for reindeer)

Emissions: Classified

Climbing Speed: One "T" (Twinkle of an eye)

Max Speed: Faster than starlight

These specs were provided by NORAD on their webpage.

Now a little bit more from the Secret Santa Files collected and correlated by NORAD.

Q) How can Santa travel the world within 24 hours?

A) NORAD intelligence reports indicate that Santa does not experience time the way we do. His trip seems to take 24 hours to us, but to Santa it might last days, weeks or even months. Santa would not want to rush the important job of delivering presents to children and spreading joy to everyone, so the only logical conclusion is that Santa somehow functions within his own time-space continuum.

Q) Does NORAD have any statistics on Santa's Sleigh?

A) NORAD can confirm that Santa's sleigh is a versatile, all weather, multi-purpose, short-takeoff and landing vehicle. It is capable of traveling vast distances without refueling and is deployed, as far as we know, only on December 24th (and sometimes briefly for a test flight about a month before Christmas.

This information will give you some ideas about how to answer questions about the sleigh, your trip and how you manage to do it all in one night.

If you go to the NORAD Tracks Santa web page, you will find a lot more answers to questions.

GLONASS Tracks Father Frost

Located in the Russian Federation is GLONASS and they track Father Frost across the Federation in real time. GLONASS is the Russian version of GPS and in part is responsible for keeping track of air flight over the Russian Federation.

This agency has been tracking the flight of Father Frost aka Ded Moroz since 2009. In 2010 on November 18th (Father Frost's Birthday) Ivan Nechayer, Executive Director of the Russian Navigation Technologies company presented Father Frost with a special staff equipped with a GLONASS navigation module in the crystal shaped top of the staff

The crystal is 180 Centimeters (7 inches) in height and weighs 3 kilograms. This module then tracks Father Frost on his journey delivering gifts.

GLONASS is the Russian answer to our NORAD where it comes to tracking their version of the Christmas time gift giver. You should note that Ded Moroz is not a version of St. Nicholas but was an evil wizard that reformed.

Candy Canes

Hard Candy has been around for a thousand years but always in a single color. The story is told of a choirmaster in 1670 was trying to think of a way to keep the children quiet during the sermon and saw these white candy sticks that lasted a long time in the hands of children.

The problem was to get the sticks into the hands of the children without upsetting the parents or causing the clergy to question this action. He asked the candy maker if the ends could be turned down in a hook like shape and thus the first candy cane was made.

To make the new "Canes" acceptable to the clergy, the choirmaster worked up a story how these were to remind the children of the shepherds that came to visit the Christ child.

The candy canes kept the children quiet during the sermon, the clergy liked the "lesson" that the canes represented and the parents like the treat their children received.

By 1770 people all across Germany were using these "Candy Canes" as Christmas tree decorations because the hook made them perfect to hang from the branches. These Canes were a big hit with adults and Children alike. Their white color was beautiful against the green of the tree and the children loved to eat the treats!

Europeans must have brought these Candy Canes to America with them but the Connection to Christmas did not become widely accepted across the country until about the mid 1840s when families started to celebrate Christmas with presents, trees and family gatherings.

It has been recorded that a German-Swedish immigrant, August Imgard was the first in the United States to use Candy Canes as ornaments. In 1847 he placed them on the fir tree he had brought into his Wooster, Ohio home for a holiday decoration. The idea quickly spread. There are many American Christmas illustrations from the second half of the 19th century showing Candy Canes as part of the holiday festivities but all of them are pictured solid white.

Red and white striped Candy Canes did not come into use until the 1920s when Bob McCormick, who ran a small confectionary in Albany, Georgia had heard of the story from England about the Candy Cane having 3 thin red stripes and 1 thick one and he made these for Christmas in his shop.

SO, the Candy Cane as we know it today has evolved over time from solid white, then red/white striped in the 1920s to the current multi-color striped and multi-flavored treats of the current year!

As has the stories about them from being a shepherds' crook with the lesson about the shepherds of the field to being a sort of "secret handshake" for Christians in England to having the Christian message expanded in the 20s with the cane being turned upside down so it becomes the letter "J" to stand for Jesus. The stories and traditions surrounding Candy Canes will likely continue to evolve and change into the future just as the flavors they come in have expanded enormously over the last 15 years! Candy Canes now come in the traditional Peppermint, Spearmint, Wintergreen, Chocolate (a favorite of the Elves), All manner of fruit flavor, Flavor changing (as the layers are licked or sucked away the flavor changes) and even Bacon flavored! As the flavors changed, so too the colors of the Canes changed as well.

Christmas Tree Lights

Martin Luther (1483-1546) is credited for having the first lit Christmas tree. He had been walking through the woods and admiring the way the stars shown through the branches at night. That inspired him to place candles on his tree at home and all that saw it admired the lit tree. The custom was copied and very soon the tradition of placing candles on the branches of Christmas trees swept across all of Germany.

This in turn started an entire new industry of craftsmen making special candleholders for use on trees and colored candles as well.

By the mid-1800s Christmas trees decorated with ornaments and lit by dozens of candles came to represent 2 things.

First it represented the "ideal" Christmas scene. Decorated and lit trees were pictured and illustrated in News Papers, Books and magazines around the world.

Second it came to represent a major fire risk! Thousands of homes were burnt to the ground due to flaming Christmas trees! Hundreds of people lost their lives in these fires!

It became such a known risk and yet the glow of a lit Christmas tree was so appealing even the families of Firemen could not be dissuaded from putting candles on their tree.

Then in 1879 Thomas Edison and his lab crew invented and developed the electric light bulb. Three years later one of

Edison's employees applied this invention to his Christmas tree.

Edward Johnson produced a string of 80 brightly colored electric bulbs and strung this string around his tree. The bulbs were much brighter than an equal number of candles and as the glow of these lights lit the room where the tree was standing it could also be seen through the large window. The neighbors began to walk by the house and marvel at the lights on the tree. As most people did not have electricity, the sight of a green tree illuminated by electric lights seemed almost magical. The fact that Johnson's lights didn't just glow but flashed on and off was quite amazing to onlookers as well.

The Detroit Post and Tribune were just the first newspapers to pay a visit to the Johnson home that Christmas.

Between the time of the Johnson's display of the new lights and the time Ralph Morris came up with the idea independently from the strings of lights used in the switchboard at his employer, New England Telephone, many wealthy families were enjoying the glow of trees lit up by electric lights. Spending as much as $3000 to outspend their neighbors with tree lights. Even the strand used by Johnson cost about $100 in materials and that was more than some families earned in a year at this time!

By 1910 GE had come out with an 8-bulb string that cost $12 but these were generally used in market windows.

It was not until after the First World War that prices dropped enough for the middle class to be able to afford these lights for their tree.

In 1924 GE and Westinghouse introduced a new set of Christmas lights that would set the industry standard for the next 50 years. These new bulbs burned cooler and lasted longer than ever before and the price dropped so that almost anyone could afford them. As power line reached the most rural areas of the country, the average American Christmas became brightly lit.

In 1923 the tradition of the national Christmas tree lighting ceremony was started by President Calvin Coolidge and continues through today. In 1933 the Rockefeller Center created another tradition with the huge tree lighting ceremony in New York City. Almost 5 centuries of lighting Christmas trees has gone on since Martin Luther lit the first candle on his tree.

Personal Encounters

I was waiting at Staples today for some printing work to be finished. Visual aids for a lecture I do and some new business cards. A small boy came up to the same counter I was waiting at and began to act out just the slightest bit with his Mom standing right behind him.

He looked at me, (I was dressed all in black from head to toe) and then continued to be a small boy. You know, eyes in the fingers, selective hearing when his mother talked to him. He was totally ignoring his mother and I could see she was a little tired so I started up a conversation with the lad as I waited. As the Mother watched carefully our conversation went like this:

M: Hello, how are you today?

LB: I am good!

M: How old are you?

LB: I am 6!

M: Oh! You're an old man!

LB: No I'm not!

M: Oh yes! It is all downhill after 5! (At this point Mom starts to smile)

LB: How come?

M: One of life's cruel jokes! You spend the first 5 years of your life getting teeth in your head and then they start to fall out! Lose any teeth lately?

LB: Smiles to show a gap and then asked, who are you?

M: I am old.

LB: What do you do?

M: A lot of things, mostly I talk to people.

LB: Oh.

M: Is that your girlfriend? (Indicating the Mother)

LB: NO!

M: Bodyguard?

LB: Yeah, sometimes you could say she is my Bodyguard. (Mom starts to chuckle)

M: Is she your Girlfriend inspector?

LB: NO!

M: Wanna bet? You bring a girlfriend home and she is going to inspect it real good! In fact I can tell you exactly what she will say.

LB: Really, what? (Mom is really listening now)

M: She will look her over real good then she will say, "Sniff! Not good enough!"

LB: (looking up at Mom) Really?

Mom: (Laughing) Yes!

M: I know these things; I had a girlfriend inspector once.

LB: Can you do magic?

M: Sometimes. It depends on what I have to do.

LB: Can you make me disappear?

M: No, because then your Mom could not see you to feed you.

While I am carrying on this conversation I show the mother some pictures of me performing on my phone.

LB: do some magic!

M: alright but first what is that? (Pointing at his shirt) LB: What? My shirt?

M: No, that! (Still pointing)

LB: Spider-man? (Pointing at the picture on the shirt)

M: No, this! (Having palmed my squeaker, I squeak his tummy)

LB: WHAAAT?!? Mom! Did you see that? (Mom is laughing again)

M: Do you always do that?

LB: No. How did you do that?

M: I am old; I am good at finding squeaky spots.

LB: Do it again!

M: Well, I guess so... (Proceed to squeak the boy in the same place again) (Mom is really laughing now)

M: (to mom) this is what I do, I bring a little surreal into their lives.

LB: Do something else! Do more magic!

M: Did you wash behind your ears today? (Palming the dollar coin in my pocket)

LB: No. Why?

M: You have something growing out of your ear.

LB: (grabbing his ear) What!!??

M: Let me get it for you. (Reach out w/ palmed coin and pull it out of his ear.)

LB: (Eyes get wide!) Mom! Did you see that? Do it again!!

M: Well pretty much cleaned that ear out.

LB: Can I have it?

M: Nope! Finders, Keepers. (Noticing a dime on the floor behind him)

LB: How about the other ear?

M: (Reaching out with the palmed coin once again) Yup! There is another one! Thanks Kid!

LB: I never find any money.

M: Turn around and look down.

LB: (Turns around and finds the dime I noticed earlier) Wow! You're good!

M: You keep that. Finders, Keepers.

LB: Can you do anything else?

M: Well when my powers are up I can do a lot.

LB: ARE YOU SANTA?

M: Does Santa wear all black?

LB: Well, no, I guess not.

M: (While he was looking down I pulled my beard out of my shirt) Want to know a little secret? (Mom is really smiling now)

LB: What?

M: (In a very quiet voice) I am Santa... have you been good?

LB: I KNEW IT! MOM!

Mom: Santa does check up on children, see?

LB: I am being good!

About then the lady's order was ready and they had to go pick up Dad. The little boy was very happy and said goodbye and the mother said thank you.

The Printer service girl said, "I can see from the photos what you do but if what you just did is any indication of the act you do, you're really great!" I thanked her for the compliment and paid for my printing that only took 3.5 hours to complete and went home.

That was how part of my day went, how was yours?

Personal Encounters
And the Blind shall see

Today I was visited by a young lady who had never sat on Santa's knee before. At the ripe old age of 9, this young lady had never had the pleasure of seeing Santa personally. Today was that day!

This little girl was blind and did not know what to expect when she sat on my knee. The Mother was somewhat anxious and apologetic while she explained her daughter was blind and had never sat with Santa before. I ask if she would like to "see" me.

The Mom was somewhat surprised at my willingness to have the girl touch my face and beard to "see" what I looked like. Once we began the girl was a little cautious but as she discovered different textures in my beard and hair, she became more confident. The glasses were next and then she had to feel the velvet and fur of my suit. Next came the boots, belt and last came the gloves.

I wear band gloves with rubber gripper dots on the palms and fingers to have a more secure grip. The little girl asked me what the gloves were saying.

Her Mother was a bit confused by that and I explained why I had the bumpy feel to my gloves and how they made sure I could maintain a good grip gently so children in my care would be safe. The little girl said, "That is nice of you to think of that."

After having been thoroughly examined and concluded the interview, I gave the girl a book but it was not in braille and she could not read it. The Mother saw my dismay at this and said to her daughter that she would have it "brailed" as soon as she got home. I think if I have more children with sight impairment visiting me this year, next year I will look into having some books in Braille handy for them as giveaways. Both Santa and the little girl learned something with this visit!

Remember to be childlike, never childish when dealing with children as Santa. It took a little bit more time to deal with the situation but the little girl, her mother and the people that were with the group were very happy with the photos that were taken. The smile on the little girl's face was well worth the effort and time to let her "see" me.

May your season be Joyous and prosperous.

Personal Encounters
More fun at the Mall for Some!

I have been at the same mall now for 3 years and have developed a sort of following with regular visitors. Some of these are mentally developed in different ways; others are physically different in their abilities. All of them love to visit with Santa and give very enthusiastic hugs! Last year the company I work for had a special pricing of $5 for a photo as a celebration of their 20 years in the business. This year the least expensive is $16.99 and with tax comes in at $18.35 for a single 5x7. I had a group of 4 ladies that wanted to have a picture with Santa but did not have the means to pay.

I am allowed a 5x7 photo for working as Santa on the set and so I used my photo to give the ladies what they so badly wanted. You see, 46% of all the people living in this city are receiving some form of assistance (2011). These are very hard times for many of those that live in San Bernardino and I very much want to give hope and joy to as many I can while I perform as Santa. This is a good thing yet I have limited resources and as the season rolls on more demands upon my time.

While I had just one free picture to do what I wished with, I have had many people asking for help in many instances. There was ONE big exception that stands out in my mind. A 12-year-old girl that came to visit with me last week. She was well-dressed and obviously well cared for with a happy smile on her face and no big demands or wishes. Her mother was a bit worn looking but obviously loved her daughter. What is so special about this little girl? She is in a wheel chair and she zips along with this big happy smile every time I see her in the mall. Her last visit, Mom lifted her from her chair and set her down on my knee to have another chat but this time it was just like all the other children, sitting on Santa's knee rather than sitting in her chair and I sitting in mine.

I finished the interview and asked the Mom if they were going to take a picture today?

The Mother looked a little pained and said "I don't have the money" and the little girl was putting a brave face on it by saying, "That's alright, I got to sit on your knee." I thought about it for maybe 30 seconds and called the photographer over and quietly told him to take a picture for the little girl and to tell the manager that I would take care of the cost.

The Mother was surprised and the little girl seemed delighted! I figured I didn't really need to have lunch that day, as my suit was a bit snug anyway. Skipped dinner too but it was worth it. Now that child has her picture and I am a little slimmer. Win/Win! I wish I could do this with every one of my "special" friends but unfortunately I can't. This must remain a rare and occasional indulgence for when my budget allows or my suit gets too snug.

Some visits are fun,

Some are sad, this one made me cry.

I have been busy all day today on this first Saturday of December. Lots of hugs and wishes listened to and photos taken. Many many happy faces sitting on my lap telling me what they desire most for Christmas.

Then a little 6-year-old girl sits down and says "All I want for Christmas is to have my mother share it with me at home".

Small warning bells are going off in my head as I look up to see both her mother and Grandmother standing by the photographer watching while we are being photographed. I ask the little girl "Where is your mother right now?" and the little girl points at the woman I thought was the Mom. I then asked, "Where will you be staying on Christmas?" thinking maybe they were going away somewhere but the little girl replies "With my Dad and Grandma".

Now I am stumped but think maybe this is a broken home situation until the girl tells me her mother will be in Afghanistan during Christmas! Now I am TOTALLY out to sea without a paddle or a compass!

I finished the photo session with the little girl and gave her a book and told her to go look at the pictures we just took. Then I called the Mom over to talk to her. I tell Mom the request of the little girl and the Mom explains she is a Navy Medic that will be going on deployment next Wed and she won't be around on Christmas. A little light is shining through but I continue to ask questions and find out Mom will be serving with an ARMY detachment as their medic. I said "ARMY?!? I knew the NAVY provided medics for the MARINES but ARMY too?"

Mom sighed and said yes this was something new and she had been given 2 weeks leave before being deployed attached to an ARMY unit. That made me think harder and faster!

I let Mom go to be with her daughter for a few minutes while they finished their transaction and then called the Mom back for a last consult. I told her of my many friends in the service that used Skype with video to stay in touch with family at home and Mom said she had just had it set up that day and taught her mother (Grandma) and daughter how to use it.

I then told Mom she could go to Hallmark and purchase one of their recordable storybooks and read the story and then leave it as a Christmas present for her daughter. That way when her daughter was home and missing mom, she could hear mom reading her a story.

Mom looked very surprised and then happy while crying at the same time and said "I am going to get one or two of those right now!" Now I wish there were something more I could do but my powers as Santa are extremely limited to holding hands and telling stories while listening to wishes.

I thanked Mom for her service, told her to be careful and to keep faith. After they left, I had to take a minute to get something out of my eye. Felt like a log or a boulder as it had me tearing up something fierce!

May God keep that little girl's Mother safe and return her whole and healthy. As the Patron Saint for all service men and women in uniform, may my prayer be heard.

Personal Encounters:
It all works out

Yesterday I had a young man (18 years old) come in with his mother to get a picture taken. He weighed 85 pounds and had palsy. We first tried to have him in his chair next to me but he kept looking to the side away from me. Then we tried him in my chair and his mother lifted him up in her arms and carried him to the Big Chair. He seemed to like that but it was too big for his safety. So we put him back in his chair and positioned him on my other side and he had the biggest smile I had ever seen! It all worked out.

I then dealt with the problems of a child that was 2 years old and blind. He saw my beard through his fingers, then the different textures of the suit from the fur to the velvet. He also checked out the gloves as well. Like any 2 year old he was a little nervous at first but with Mom there with him, it all worked out.

Then it was on to the little boy (5 years old) whose father was in jail. His older cousin (9 years old) was here but her father was living in Mexico and could not come up to see her anymore. We talked about how sometimes Daddys made mistakes but they always loved their children. With a hug and listening to a few requests, it all worked out.

Later I had a family that was living in a motel room. Their house had burned down and the children were worried that I would not find them Christmas Eve. A few hug, a couple of stories and it all worked out.

Last I had a little girl who asked for her mother to be home for Christmas. We talked about her Aunt that had escorted her to visit me and so I waived the Aunt over. The little girl and I joke about how her "ant" didn't have 6 legs, and she wasn't all red, and she didn't live in an ant farm. We were all laughing about that and then we talked about the little girl's mother. Mom was in Cedars Sinai Hospital with leukemia. I immediately assured the little girl that her mother was in one of the VERY BEST places to be as an adult! I also told her that not even Santa could contradict the orders of the doctors treating her Mother but that I would do everything I could to help her see her mother on Christmas Day. After the Aunt sent her to look at the pictures, we talked quietly about the Mom and what was happening. For the little girl it all worked out.

I see many children every day while I am sitting in the mall. Most of them just want to give me their requests for toys and get a hug. They are cherished and given the due attention that is expected from Santa when he is busy. Then there are the Children that take a little more time and effort to care for. I spend as much time as needed to make sure they are as happy and secure as I can facilitate.

Sometimes that gets me a fishy stare from my manager for taking too long, but then I explain why and it all works out.

The Delivery Man

Eight short stories highlighting 24 years of Delivering Christmas to Family Homes

By Bertram Gordon Bailey
RBS

Dedication

This book is dedicated to all the Delivery Men that give up their home and Family life to serve as Santa to all the communities they serve. May your eyes twinkle, may your visits be Jolly and may your travels be safe on Christmas Eve.

Your work to preserve the Secret of Santa for children everywhere is a labor of love and dedication to the Spirit of Christmas everywhere bringing Hope, Love, Peace, Joy and Happiness to children around the world.

Santa Bertram Gordon Bailey

RBS

Foreword

I have been a Delivery Man on Christmas Eve since 1980 visiting families in their homes, Hospitals, Convalescent homes.

Anywhere I get the call to appear. While I have visited thousands of Families and many thousands of children, these eight stories are like gems that sparkle and stand out as memorable to me and happened on Christmas Eve except for one that happened at the end of a hot summer. Each one highlights an important lesson I learned along my journey in becoming a Delivery Man for Santa spanning the time between 1983 through 2007.

Starting in 2008 I became a Mall Santa or what we call a High Volume Vendor Santa and that is an entirely different pack of stories all together!

These Short stories are here now for your enjoyment!

Thank you for reading them, only the names have been changed to protect the privacy of the people involved.

Santa Bertram Gordon Bailey

RBS

Contents

The Delivery Man

It is dark and raining now. I have been on the road making deliveries since morning and I still have 3 stops to go before my route is done today. The radio is playing loudly to keep me company and help keep me alert as I drive. It also keeps me aware of the time and traffic during this storm.

As I drive up Vineyard Blvd. the water is almost a river streaming down hill making it safer to drive up the inside lane as the outside lane is under a foot or two of running water. As I approach the address, I wonder again what it is that keeps me going away from home and family on this night of all nights. It is the same every year, only the faces and addresses change mostly.

Because of the rain and the traffic caused by it, I am running a little late and with each stop on the schedule, I become a bit later as the lag accumulates and yet every stop off seems to be pleasing to those that I make the delivery to. Some are surprised I made their drop off at all due to the storm. I just tell them I get there eventually no matter what the circumstances.

I ease the truck over to the curb as I reach my destination. Unfortunately the rain has decided to downpour harder now and even the driver's side tires are in 6 inches of running water. I can barely see the house through the pounding rain and it is only 20 yards or so away, yet the porch light is on and there are cars in the driveway. Taking a minute to shelter in the truck in hopes that the rain will subside proves fruitless. Time is passing and I am already late.

I get out and put on the coat and belt that is part of the delivery uniform and place my hat on my head. Thank goodness for the boots I have to wear! They at least are waterproof and come higher than the running water! I grab the delivery bag and make my way to the home where I see more packages waiting to be delivered wrapped in plastic bags to keep them out of the rain. Foregoing the usual transfer of packages from where they sit to the bag, I simply pick up the bundles and place them in my bag and then after a quick check of the uniform (Yup! All there even if I am now dripping wet through and through) I knock on the door to make my delivery that the children are eagerly waiting for!

A tired and harried looking woman answers my knock and says "Thank God you're here! We were worried you wouldn't make it through the storm!!" and then she notices how wet I am with water dripping off my hat and uniform and she hands me a towel and welcomes me into the warmth and light of the home. After I mop my face and dry my glasses I reply "Ho Ho Ho! What? Me miss this visit and disappoint the children? Nonsense!" and I then proceed to find the "Chair" and as I sit down, all the rain, the wet, the tiring schedule is forgotten and once again I am Santa!

After a wonderful visit with the giving of gifts, answering children's questions and taking of photos my hostess ends the visit on time, giving up a few minute she had paid for to help me get back on schedule along with a nice cup of hot tea and a cookie it's back on the road again for I have 3 more deliveries to make tonight!

An Orthodox Delivery

It is New Year's Eve and normally I would be home warm, safe and happily playing with my one Christmas gift that I give to myself each year.

However a call was placed for a delivery and I answered the call as always. This time it is to the hills west of Hollywood through a tangled maze of housing streets to a home that amazingly had snow on the yard!

I pull the truck over a couple of houses up from the address and survey the area since I arrived with time to spare. Wooded lots, nice homes and no children about. Curious but it is getting on to dusk and the weather had been cold, perhaps they were all inside where it was warm.

No matter, I get out of the truck and put on the coat and hat. Buckle the belt and pick up my bag to make the delivery. I come to the porch but there are no packages, just a letter. Several letters but the cover is from the Mother explaining the nature of the visit. All the other letters are from the children of the house wishing me well and in hopes that I have had a wonderful year before they list the objects of their desire.

The Mother's letter had already explained the gifts they sought were already under the tree as well as the praise worthy events of the last year with annotations on the children's letters on what to have each child possibly work on in the coming year.

I knock on the door and am welcomed in. A young boy has my hand and leads me to the couch next to his

Grandmother and we all sit to discuss their letters and accomplishments.

Throughout this time the Grandmother continues to smile and occasionally clap her hands in the joy of watching the children.

My young guide has made himself my helper for the duration, bringing me presents and helping me with the name pronunciations. Every child receives several gifts along with the "Most Important" one mentioned in their letters. Grandmother is just as excited as any of the children with each presentation clapping her hands, smiling and the occasional laugh.

The time goes by faster than I expected and then the last gift is handed to me by my assisting honorary elf. It is for Grandmother, the lady that has not said so much as a word to me yet has smiled and cheered along with all the children.

With a look of surprise and wonder she opens the brightly wrapped and beribboned gift with trembling hands and a little help from my helper. Inside the box is an antique porcelain doll of great beauty. Grandmother looks at me with watery eyes but a small smile on her face and gives me a pat on the shoulder.

Shortly after that it is time to go and as I am escorted out by the Mother, she too is crying. She explains to me her mother was in the advanced stages of dementia and had not interacted with anyone in the family for months. Until I had walked through the door the old woman had done nothing but sit on the couch and ignored all that happened around her. I had wondered why the other adults were so quiet while the children; Grandmother and I were having such a wonderful time.

The Mother thanked me for helping bring her mother back to her for one last Christmas. Yes, I said Christmas for this was their Christmas Eve as they were Orthodox Catholic and my visit was so very important to their celebration, this year more than ever.

Sometimes the gifts I deliver are not in the bag or wrapped in pretty paper. Sometimes it is simple faith and hope that I deliver.

A Delivery of Small Importance

For some time now, I have been working as a Deliveryman and thought I had seen most every kind of package to take to someone. I was wrong.

The "Special Request" for this delivery was to bring as many candy canes as I could manage! No quantity listed, just "lots!" were required for this drop off. So I loaded my belt with 60, put another 3 dozen in my little bag and even carried a few boxes of the sweets in with me on this run.

The drop off address was a nursing home. I had never been into a nursing home but I was told there would be a guide to inform me as to what was required. As I entered the reception desk lady exclaimed "Good! You're here!" and I was instructed to "Wait right there!" as she ran off to fetch the person that had ordered the delivery.

The activities manager then came out and looked me over and said "You'll do!" and took me back to the auditorium where there were all these families waiting for me. Children, young adults, middle-aged couples and old adults that were in the care of their families were all sitting and waiting for me.

I was brought to a chair and once seated the families came up to sit on my knee and tell me their desires. I in turn gave each and every one a candy cane and my best holiday wishes.

After the groups had had their chance to sit with me and received their canes, I had to go back out to the truck and resupply for the second half of the delivery, that of going room to room for the residents that were shut in.

These visits were a bit more interesting as these folks had no one to visit with them and so I would give them a candy cane and then talk about the weather outside, the clouds in the blue sky, the flowers and trees all full of color now that it was fall. The smell of the rain coming and the chill of the coming of autumn.

Many of these would ask for a second cane, as the food was so "Bland" and after a nod from my guide, I would grant them their wish with a smile and a hug.

My final visit was with a very small and thin lady that had very bright eyes but no teeth! She asked me if I knew "How Candy Canes and Bananas were alike?" well I puzzled that one for a few seconds and then gave up. She told me "They both taste better when you peel them!" I then peeled her cane for her and left her with all I had left on me. Her bright outlook and cheerful sharing of a joke was such a gift to me! I learned that I not only deliver, but receive as well.

Special Delivery!

I am up at 5:30 in the morning to make a Special Delivery today! I got in form my deliveries late last night, or was it early this morning? Then I recall I was lying down at 2 am to catch a nap after my deliveries of yesterday after a cold meal and a hot drink. Three and a half hours, no wonder my eyes feel gritty. Well at least the uniform is dry and I am reasonable awake!

I arrive with the dawn to meet a father dressed in slippers and a bathrobe holding a paper and cup of coffee waiting for me out in front of the home. As I put the coat and belt on, place the hat on my head and pull out my bag, he goes to a SUV and waits there for me to walk over. "Thank you for doing this so early! These little guys have been waiting all night out here and the children have no idea what is coming!" he tells me. I look in to find two small Golden Retriever puppies about 8 weeks old squirming with excitement! I look at the bag, then at the puppies that are obviously excited and tell the father "I had better hold these packages in my hands because putting them in a bag might just distress them." And he agrees taking my bag and placing it on the chair out on the porch for me to collect as I leave.

As the Father slips in through the door he asks me to "give me a couple of minutes to get into the bedroom and then knock" and I agree. Standing there with wriggling puppies in each hand I do the only thing I can, I gently kick the door with my boot!

It takes a couple of tries to wake the children and then through the door I hear "Dad! There is someone at the door!" and the Father replies, "Well find out who it is and let them in!"

The door opens to show twin girls dressed in PJs looking sleepy for only an instant then they see Santa standing there! Eyes open wide with squeals of delight the children are yelling for their parents to come!

I ask them if I might come in and the girls grab my coat and proceed to guide/drag me into their home. The parents, the Father still in his bathrobe and the Mother just out of bed with her bathrobe belted tightly, watch as their children practically bounce off the walls! As I walk in I quickly survey the home and note the pairs of shoes left in a cubby by the door and the very large and beautifully decorated tree dominating the living room. I also note several dog centric items had been left on the mantelpiece that the children had not noticed yet.

The first hurdle was when the children asked, "Which one is mine?" in stereo. I replied, "Let's sit down and let them choose who their girl is instead?" That was immediately followed by the "Plop" of small bottoms hitting the floor! Then before I turned the puppies loose into their new environment and to the care of their new owners, I cautioned the girls to take good care of the pups. "They do not know the rules here yet and you have shoe to chew and a nice tree for indoor plumbing for them. You will have to care for these two because they are living creatures that will give you endless love. Never allow your selves to become angry with them but guide them when they do something wrong." The girls promised to take excellent care of their new charges and I released the hounds! As luck would have it, the puppies decided to go to a single girl each. Each young lady was completely enchanted with their treasure and I was soon forgotten.

Such is life as a deliveryman!

A Surprise Delivery!

I am the Delivery Man and normally I deliver packages along with a bit of surreal and humor, Joy, Hope and Faith. But this was to be the Biggest Delivery of my entire career! For I was to deliver an entire Christmas!

One of my usual route Directors came to me with a special request. She had heard of a family that was struggling. The Grandmother had taken both her son and her daughter and two grandsons back into her home/condo due to troubles related to the down turn in the local economy.

This Director had heard about this family and asked if I would make a special surprise delivery for her. When informed what was to be delivered the Director then asked what I would need to do this on Christmas morning.

Well I thought hard about getting up early after getting back to home and hearth at 3 am the night before, the cost of the fuel, my time away from home on this day for Family then stacked that up against what the family I would be delivering to would receive and what it would mean to those two boys. I told her "Nothing".

Well come the day, I was at the appointed location parked around the corner and out of sight of the home. The Director drove up and thanked me for doing this for her. I then got into my coat, buckled my belt and placed my hat upon my head only to find not one large bulging bag, but TWO! One Red, one Green.

Grabbing a bag at the top in each gloved hand, I pulled them up and over my shoulders then proceeded to walk around the corner loaded down with the gift of the Holiday! Once I got to the door, the home was quiet and I realized I had once again no hands to knock, as with the Puppy delivery done a few years before. So I used the same solution and gently kicked the door. Immediately the sound of a large dog barking came from the other side.

A few minutes went by so I kicked the door again a bit more firmly and again the dog did his best to defend the family by barking! It was at this point a young lady in a bathrobe and tired but angry eyes opened the door to yell "What do you want?!?" but by the time the last word escaped her, her eyes had gone round and her mouth dropped open! Seems NO ONE in the home knew I was coming except the Grandmother and she did not know what it was that I was bringing in detail.

I apologized for kicking the door but as she could see my hands were rather full. The young mother backed into the home and I entered. There was a tree and a large flat screen in an obviously mature person's home with little evidence that children lived there beyond a couple of toys that had been opened the night before. It was a rather sparse display of Christmas cheer that I was sent to rectify.

The German shepherd was friendly enough with a wagging tail but the Mother was still unsure as to my intentions. She asked me more than once if I had the right address. I asked if the boys resided here and mentioned them by name and that seemed to assure her that indeed I was at the right place but she was completely puzzled as to why or how I came to be there so early on Christmas Morning.

I was lead to the dining room/kitchen/stairway area (this was a rather small condo for 5 people but quite cozy for one retired Grandma) where I found a stool to sit on to hand out the gifts. I told the mother that I would explain all but it would be better if the rest of the family was there to hear the story as well. The Mother yelled up the stairs "MOM! Kids! Get down here!" and so there arrived a short parade of sleepy eyed children, an older woman dressed in a worn bathrobe and a half dressed young man in his twenties that had to be the brother. All but the Grandmother looked on in wonder as I introduced myself.

The stairs became stadium seating as I opened the Green Bag first as per my instructions. There to the mother I gave a basket of comfort items including bath salts, candles, a new robe, hair care and some simple make up supplies, a gift card for groceries, a gift card for gas, and tickets to the movie theater for her and the boys along with a box of chocolates.

I had no idea what was in the bags so these gifts of largess were just as much a surprise to me as to them! The next thing pulled from the Green bag was a basket for Grandma. Again it contained comfort items with a new robe, bath items, Skin crème and moisturizer, A pass to a spa for two, a gift card for a clothing store that would work for everyone in the family, an envelope with a voucher from a local restaurant for a complete dinner from soup to dessert for 8 (leftovers) ready to be picked up any time after 1 pm that day and copious amounts of fine chocolate.

The next item explained why the dog accepted me so quickly, for out came a box of Milk bones a bag of kibble along with a nice ball! Then a large can of mixed nuts! Yes I had brought Christmas dinner to the family complete from soup to nuts!

The director seemed to have thought of everything! Near the bottom of the Green Bag there was also some video of Christmas movies!

Then I dragged the Red bag into view and the two boys got excited! From within I pulled out a Radio Control car complete with batteries with the first boy's name on it, then a second exactly like the first but in a different color for the second child! Then a third one for the Uncle! That woke him up! Next came shirts for all three men (uncle and both boys) more gift cards to Toys R Us for all three, A gas card for Uncle, a gift card for a shoe store and a large basket filled with microwave popcorn, candy and snacks for each of them! Movie tickets for their uncle were at the bottom of the Red Bag.

Now perhaps because the Director was a lady, there was more attention to detail for the gifts to the ladies I was visiting for they certainly seemed to have made the right impression! Boys being boys, the toys and clothes seemed to be satisfactory for the three of them, especially the snacks!

Following the gift giving I shared some stories of Christmas and listened to the children for their wishes for the coming year and next Christmas. Then after what seemed to be only 15 minutes but turned out to be 90, I made my way to leave. I left the bags behind as per instructions.

Before I was even half way down the driveway, one of the boys came running out in his bare feet and PJs yelling "You forgot your bags!" and I told him "I did forget, they were left to remind them both that Santa cares year round!" He went back inside holding the two bags as if they were the finest gift ever presented.

When I got back to my truck I found an envelope had been slipped through the crack of my window sitting on the seat. Inside was a card that said "Thank you for giving up your rest and morning!" and though I had said I would do this for no charge and was feeling better for it walking back to the truck, the gift inside was very nice as well.

Sometimes it isn't the packages I deliver as much as the wonder of having everything a Christmas should have in the morning after going to bed the night before with little to look forward to. The Grandmother was doing the best she could for her own and this "Gift of the Magi" was what it took to put the wonder of the season back into her eyes as well as the rest of the family. "God Bless us, Everyone!"

The Delivery Man keeps them Flying!

I have other jobs during the year besides delivering packages during the Season. At one point for several years I would deliver tanks of Helium to car dealerships and banks.

Delivering Helium is a dirty and sweaty job during the summer when the vehicle has no air conditioning and the windows don't roll down all around the van. The tanks are heavy and kind of dirty as well. During the summer as you hustle the tanks in and out of the van you get pretty grubby looking with salt rings on your shirt from all the sweat drying as you drive. I know, not a pretty image.

One stop was at a car dealership in Redlands California at about 4 in the afternoon in the middle of summer. I had been out since morning and this was the 6th of 7th city on today's run.

As I was rolling the latest 242cf tank in through the lobby on the handcart a child looked up and yelled "Hey Santa! What are you doing here!?"

I recognized the family as one of the visits I had done last Christmas and thought fast as the father smiled and the mother frowned.

A bit of quick thinking had the answer, now to see if it would be accepted by the child, "You know how my Reindeer fly around the world on Christmas Eve?" I asked and he nodded his little head. "Well I am going to let you in on a little secret, but you can't tell anyone!" The child agreed to this but the Father and Mother now looked a bit concerned. A couple of the sales men had gathered to listen as well.

"You see this tank? It holds the Helium that makes balloons float in the air." One of the salesmen brought the boy a balloon that he held tightly while nodding his head. "I preposition extra tanks of Helium along the path of my route in case I have to "Top Off" one or more of the Reindeer to keep them flying!"

You could see the little wheels turning in his head as he thought about my answer and then nodded saying "Yeah, that makes sense!" The salesmen were chuckling, the Father was laughing but the Mother while laughing said "Eewww! That's disgusting!"

With a nod and a wink to the child, I stood up and went back to work! Got to keep them flying Proud and High!

Sometimes you will be recognized even in the middle of summer not looking your best due to your work. It matters not how you look, what matters is you were indeed recognized and must slip into character for the sake of the child.

By giving him a reason for my being there instead of the North Pole and why I was moving large tanks of Helium about, I introduced a bit of surreal into the lives of the Parents and gave the child the gift of Believing for a while longer.

The 24th Delivery

2007 and 24 years have passed since I made my first delivery to this family on Christmas Eve and it has shown in many ways over the years of visits. Foreign Exchange students shared the joy with the Family 3 times now. Once from Japan, once from the Ukraine and once from Bolivia which rounded out the crowd between births.

Over that time my "uniform" went through some changes and no longer smelled of wet dog when it rained as well as my overall appearance but for this Family I was the Delivery Man.

That first year there were two adorable blond twin girls about 4 years old. To one I gave a Kitchen play set complete with counter and sink. To the other I brought an "Easy Bake Oven" and they were to share.

Throughout the years the Clan would gather together on that very Special night and wait for the Delivery Man to arrive. Some years were lean while other years were prosperous but all came to share the warmth of the season and to see what was to be delivered to each of them this year…

The bag was heavily weighted with gifts both numerous and varied. The younger members had several packages of all size and weight while the older members would have one or two very meaningful packages to smile and sigh over. Since the Clan was large and the packages were many, I dispensed with the usual Gossip of how the year went by for everyone and get down to the heart of the delivery as far as those young ones are concerned!

There is something comical in watching a 4 year old struggling to carry off a package both bigger than and nearly as heavy as she is. So too the embarrassment of a teenager coming to sit on the knee of the Delivery Man to collect a very small, flat envelope but the smile that wreaths their faces and the exclamations of Joy when they open them are very nearly identical.

Normally this particular delivery stop is fairly well organized and follows the schedule starting with the Children first and finishing up with the Adults with some quiet conversation as we survey the destruction of wrapping paper and ribbons.

This time however a change occurred. About 10 minutes into the package deliveries, a lovely blond woman walks up and sits down on my knee without being called. At a guess I thought she must be around 28 years of age and rather healthy as she bounced up and down, side to side on my knee while saying "See? Santa is nice! Santa won't hurt you! Mommy likes Santa!" to a small girl about 3 years of age with a doubtful expression on her face.

I thought back but it had been about 5 years since I last saw this young woman and I did not see her sister this year so

I could not put my finger on her name. Sitting back, I said, "You know, it has been so long now that I can't remember if it was you I gave the Easy Bake Oven to or your sister."

Well, the woman froze with her back perfectly straight! She slowly turned her head to look carefully at my face and asked, "That was You?!?" to which I replied "It has been me every year my dear, I am so happy to meet your daughter and to be introduced to her in such a friendly fashion!"

At this point the little girl slowly and cautiously comes up to take her Mothers hand and peer around her to look up at me. She then looks up at her Mother sitting quietly on my knee now as if to ask, "Really?" before taking the gift I had for her. A small Teddy Bear.

Running off hugging the bear to hide behind "Grandpa" it was not long before her name was called again and she ran up to receive her second package of the delivery in good form. Thus another generation formed another link in the chain of deliveries.
Then when the last package was delivered and the last conversation was finished, the Matriarch (that had originally arranged that first delivery so long ago), the Grandma and the blond young Mother all walked me out the door to ensure no small eyes observed my departure and gave me the best gift of all, a hug from three generations for being so kind to the newest generation of the family.

That hug, along with a plate of cookies still warm from the oven went a long way to keeping me warm on that cold night as I went on to finish my rounds.

The Last Delivery

Someday in your time delivering packages, you may be called to make a "Last Delivery" to a home. I received one such call to go to a long time home visit address to see Jon.

Jon was a happy, inquisitive and enthusiastic boy of about 4 that I had delivered to on Christmas Eve for about 10 years running. When I first met Jon he was near 8 years of age and though his body grew over time, he remained 4 in his life.

That first year it was the Parents, Aunt and Uncle, and the Grandparents there in the small apartment when I arrived. Jon was excited and would lose control of his arms and legs when so much excitement happened around him but he was a sweet lad!

I delivered the packages and told stories then posed for pictures with Jon with a concerned Mother hovering nearby as I held Jon in my arms on my knee. His smile was a wonderful gift that year and one I shall always remember for as long as I can

Like many of my long-term delivery customers, this family moved around over the years always upwardly as their fortunes and families grew. Jon grew as well.

Other children came along as families split and then blended as this often happens and over time Jon had three cousins that would visit on this special night as well as the clan grew. About 8 years along I brought a "Hear and Say" for Jon that you placed the pointer on a picture and pulled the string and the device would say, "Cow! The Cow goes

Mooo!" with a different message for each picture. Jon really liked the cow though.

Jon was still 4 but his body had grown to that of a tall and strong near adult but without the fine motor skills that would let him sit or stand still. He was also noticing that while he was loved, his cousins were maturing leaving him behind mentally and physically as they too grew. They also received different gifts that were unfortunately far more fragile. Jon would become angry over this but when I arrived his smile and excitement was always very plain to see.

He would jump up and come to me where I was sitting and drop right on my knee. All 170 pounds of him in the excitement and joy of a 4 year old. His parents were always nearby and watchful but Jon wanted to show them he was "big" too.

I was able to keep Jon steady despite his size and strength but when our time was done and it was time for the first cousin he became rather angry. Later the Father took me aside and explained they had been working with Jon with specialists but he had grown too strong and lashed out in anger often that he might have to be placed in a facility that could both deal with this child in a grown up body and help Jon reach his full potential.

The following year I saw Jon again he was greatly changed! His manners were much better and his coordination was as well. That year I learned from the Father that Jon was responding well to medication and the intensive one on one therapy. When Jon came over and sat on my knee that year, though his coordination was better, the landing on the knee was the same! Plop! His mother always winced but I just bounced Jon as always.

The next year was the last. Jon's body simply could not deal with the constant trials his ailment placed upon him and his anger would not let him find peace. Earlier that year toward the end of summer Jon left this world for a better one where Jon would be whole and well.

There was a dark pall over the family gathering as they all quietly sat around remembering Jon. I delivered the packages and chatted with the children that were now entering Middle school in some cases or finishing Elementary. Jon's Mother was very sad and his Father was doing what he could to keep the family together.

That visit was my last but the children there were well cared for and they enjoyed their time sitting on my knee (except the oldest) and I went out into the dark night to complete my rounds thinking of and remembering Jon. And the Cow.

A Delivery Man cannot bring back what was lost but he can stand and remember those that have left. He can help those in pain remember the happier times and in delivering those memories, ease the burden of loss.

Afterword

I have been doing this delivery work for well over more time than I can clearly remember. My time has spanned Children, Grandchildren, and Great-grandchildren through multiple generations of hundreds of families.

My strength is leaving me, as is my memory. The spirit is willing but there comes a time to realize my journey is coming to an end but before that last delivery I have gifts to impart to you.

Though my journey has been long and sometimes the thing that drives me on is not understood by family or loved ones, it is a journey that I share with you. Others like myself that put on the Red Delivery Suit and go out into the cold night to deliver those valuable packages to those that have loved ones as well. Especially on that very special night on December 24th.

The first gift is Humility. This job is not about You or Me. Rather it is about the Spirit of the season. The Giving of one's self to others without thought of self-importance. As Santa we are both Famous yet anonymous because none of us is the real Santa. All are Delivery Men.

You deliver the gifts and the Joy that those gifts bring to those they are meant for. Not for any other reason beyond that of the second Gift. The second Gift is Joy, for where ever you go; whenever you wear the Red Suit that is our uniform you bring the Joy of the season with you. Not just the gifts in the bulging bag, but with the care, and words you bring as well.

The third Gift is Hope, for we bring the hope for a brighter future and the promise to children everywhere that there is indeed someone in the world that cares for them simply because they are here in this world.

The last Gift is Faith. We give the others we visit that Faith is here in our hearts and we share that Faith in our service. The children have Faith that the Delivery Man will come through with the visit no matter what the weather or how we may personally feel at any one time. We keep that Faith with our dedication to our charges.

If you keep your Humility and share the Joy, Hope and Faith of the season, then you will be richly rewarded indeed!

But if the job is secondary to your self-importance, to your financial reward, this will not be the job for you and you will soon enough find a new path to those rewards you seek.

The season was never about the Delivery Man but about the Gifts of the season and how those gifts can help people get through the darkest time of the year. It is about maintaining that Spark in the Hearts of others all the year round.

And when the children we visit in turn have children of their own, they continue the tradition of the delivery of gifts that are wrapped up in that Hope, Joy and Faith that nurtures the spark in the next small generation to follow. And so it goes.

My final gift is to myself as I wrap my mind with the warm memories of families and children I have visited to stave of the chill of old age until it is time for my last delivery to the next world. I will not be the Delivery Man then, only the delivered.

Santa Bertram Gordon Bailey

RBS

Flowers for Algernon

Afterword

"Everything we have in life is on loan,

Even the food we eat." Harry Anderson

"The secret to being a great children's entertainer is,

Be Childlike not childish!" Roberta Doggett

"If you can dream it,

You can do it." Walt Disney

"We must select the illusion which appeals to our temperament, and embrace it with passion."

Cyril Connolly

"If I had known I was going to live this long,

I'd have taken better care of myself!" Mickey Mantle

"I have a mind to join a club and beat you over the head with it." Rufus T. Firefly

"Always remember the Golden Rule son,

He who has the Gold, makes the rules." Bert Bailey Sr.

"Smile and wave boys, Smile and wave."

The Penguin in Madagascar

The way to use this book is with your imagination, heart and desire to become the best Santa/performer you can be. Everyone starts from the same point, the beginning, but how they start and with what kind of support is another story. If you have the desire and the drive, it may take a bit longer than someone that has money as well but you will get there eventually.

This textbook and the other two that go with it to form the base of the "Santa and the Business of being Santa" Santa school will give you Information on the Business side of being an independent contractor entertainer, Connections to the people that support us and hire us to do this job of Santa, the basic grounding in the Performance of being Santa and Some of the history of the Character and the traditions that influenced the shape and form of the role today.

Some of the things that will make the journey easier and move quicker along would be to join a local group of Santas that would allow you to learn from their experience. Find a "Mentor" Santa that will take you under his guidance and teach you the ins and outs of the business. Attend as many gatherings as you can fit in during the year. Attend as many Santa schools as you can afford and simply listen and absorb as much information as you can. Purchase such books as Tim Connaghan's "Behind the Red Suit", Victor Nevada's book on being Santa or any of my own offerings. Search through Amazon for others that offer advice on being Santa. All of this will help you become the best Santa you can be in as short a time as possible. Then you too will be looked upon as a Santa "mentor" in your time and it will be your turn to pass along not only the information given to you but that which you learned from hard experience to the next wave of Santas.

Perhaps in time you too will become a School owner and instructor. It has become a very competitive field lately and rather crowded but those that have the drive and sincere wish to help others in becoming better than they are presently, operating a Santa School has become a new kind of venue for at least 14 new school owners since this school started since 2014 to this writing in 2015.

When it comes to Suits and Boots, gather the best quality you can afford each time you are in the market to upgrade. A Halco Velvet suit or a Rubies #2354 fully lined Velvet suit will last you at least a decade of heavy wear. A pair of Round Heel Ropers make a fine pair of boots to start with and should last you at least 5 years of performance.

When you are ready to upgrade, then it is time to look at Speir's Specialty Boots or the equivalent, an Adele's suit would be the next step or one like it. Starting out takes money and you will spend $600 to $800 outfitting yourself easily but then your next upgrade will cost you around $700 to $800 for the upgrade top end boots and the Suit will set you back around $1500 for the full basic top of the line set up. This level of gear will last you around 15 to 20 years with care. Yes the cost is high but the amortized cost per year is far less than repurchasing the cheapest suit several times each year.

When you are educating yourself about performance, look at local Junior College opportunities for attending a theater class to learn more about performing, Take a class on Improvisation and Comedy. Practice your story telling by reading to your Grandchildren and offering your services as a story teller to your local Library, Book store and your local Boys and Girls club.

Join a Story telling group in your area, join a speakers club as well. Cultivate a friendship/relationship with several Costume rental outlets and Costume sale shops in your area.

Network with the Santas in your area as much as possible as they will give you work they cannot do themselves because they are already booked.

Finally get your business cards and always carry them in your wallet ready to hand out to anyone that asks, "Do you play Santa?" Get some tri-fold flyers with your pictures and information on your performance including your rates and then go out and contact every Car dealership, Hotel, Large market and Mall in comfortable driving distance and speak with the Marketing manager, the Sales Promotion manager, the advertising manager and also contact any military base in your area and ask to talk to the MWR manager. This will help you find work. When you do a party, be sure to give everyone 2 of your business cards. One for them to keep and one to give to a friend.

When you take the classes, join the groups, volunteer to read at the library/book store or volunteer to do pictures at the local pet store/shelter, in fact anything you do to become Santa you will be making friends.

Learn to Network with these friends to locate more jobs for your Santa presentation. Every performance will add to your experience base and this in turn will quickly make you a seasoned professional. Most important, always remain in character even after the work is done for so long as you are still in the suit. Once you are home and changed out of your suit, then you can relax from the "Santa" character. Maintain your equipment in top shape at all times as you never know when you may get the call to do "Santa in the summer" or have a call for a photo shoot. Maintain your beard in a neat manner and always be clean and groomed when out in the public in or out of season. My advice and this school deals in today's reality of the market and what is changing in it. If you bought this book or any of my text books you then value these words. You value them even more if you attend one of my classes.

Back in the late 90s and early 2000s it was very possible to land a mall job that paid $30,000. Those that could spin their own PR could and did walk into Bass Pro Shops and made as much as $22,000 in the mid-2000s.

Sadly those are the "Good old Days" and the reality is this. Small and medium sized malls have no budget to add for hiring a Santa. Large Malls still have a budget but even those have curtailed their spending since the economic crash of 2008. Many Photo companies will pay you $12,500 for a 49 day contract that will see you on site for an average of 600 hours +/- 5% and at that rate you are making $25 an hour.

They are now expecting you to pay for your travel and housing out of that. That can run around $4000 and more for the season not including airfare. The best you can do is go into negotiations with an understanding of what you are facing and what the Photo company values most in a Santa performer.

Last but not least, when doing this work always remember to Have Fun!!!

Thank you for reading this work and my other books if you have them.

Santa Gordon Bailey

SatBobS.com

After note:

As of 2015 WWP had a corporate buy out and has since in 2017 decided to pay for housing and transportation once again in part because of the 2016 season with the shortage of Real Beard Santas. In 2016 both Cherry Hill and Noerr were bought out and then merged by a parent company. Due to this Noerr had to recall all their contracts and rewrite them naming those that worked for them as Independent Contractor Entertainers. That merged company also had problems with the "Santa Shortage" of 2016.

A result of this is the mall photo companies have been signing contracts for the 2017 season as of February 1. A very early time when normally they are finishing up in June with this.
Additionally, in 2016 Bass Pro Shop bought out the Cabellas chain of stores for $5.5 Billion. There were more Cabellas stores than Bass Pro Shops and those stores will start to be converted over to the BPS model starting in February 2017. Each will have a "Santa's Winter Wonderland" hiring 2 Santas.

This alone will tighten the market for performing Santas but if the "Big Box" stores enter in again as they did in 2016, there will be far more designer bearded Santas working chairs as there will again be a shortage of Real Beard Santas to cover the demand.

My advice to all is this. If you are looking to maximize the earnings you can make and have the basics of the equipment and skill/talents needed you will work home visit and corporate visit. You will have to hustle but you can do 100 visits a season if you do. Those of you that wish to work a Mall or High Volume Venue, you should be able to negotiate in 2017 a better deal than in 2016 simply because they anticipate a tighter supply. In other words it is a seller's market.

In every case, it would pay you to look at what is happening to our industry beyond what is right in front of you. The landscape is always shifting and the people that keep their balance in adapting to the changes as they happen will always do better than those that continue to live in "The Good Old Days". Observe what is happening to the people/agencies/Photo companies that hire us. Pay attention to the economy both in your region and the Nation to get a feel for what is going to affect the industry in the coming months.

International hiring contract are in a stage of shift and change as well. Do your research and due diligence before you sign those contracts. Failure to do so will cause you terrible experiences from which come better decisions. Far better to avoid the bad experience by paying attention today.

Made in the
USA
Middletown, DE